ONE MAN'S ROSES

One Man's Roses

Tales from Uncle Sol's Neighborhood

Renee U. Garrett

Illustrated by Andrea S. Hand

Quiet Waters Publications
2011

Copyright ©2011 by Renee U. Garrett. All rights reserved. No part of this book may be used or reproduced in any manner without written permission, except in the case of brief quotations embodied in critical articles and reviews.

Illustrated by Andrea S. Hand. www.andreahand.com

For information contact:
    Quiet Waters Publications
For prices and order information visit:
    http://www.quietwaterspub.com

Scripture taken from The Message. Copyright 1993, 1994, 1995, 1996, 2000, 2001, 2002. Used by permission of NavPress Publishing Group.

ISBN 978-1-962698-17-7
Library of Congress Control Number: 2010940985

2nd printing 20110221
3rd printing 20250428

Dedicated to the beloved men in my life:

Rex
Spencer
Peter
and
Tyler

Imagine a place
Filled with happy sounds of playgrounds
Where every child is safe
Where people join hands
And pray that the children will all have a chance
In every family, every tribe and every town
We're the keepers of the garden and we can't let them down,
They are the roses
They are the lights that shine
They are the waves that roll in on the ocean tide
They are angels
They are souls in flight
They are the hopes that everything's gonna be alright
They are the roses

Randy Van Warmer, Tim Schoept, Paul Jenkins
"They Are The Roses"

Contents

Acknowledgements 11
Introduction 14

The Stories
   A Drop of Faith 17
   Team Effort 22
   Kite Calamity 27
   Lemonade Wisdom 37
   Inner Change 41
   A New Home for Christmas 47
   An Unexpected Flower 53
   The Secret Artist 63
   Trusting the Clues 68
   Seeing the Truth 75
   The Boy Who Would be King 83
   The Sliding Hill 91
   Patina Sisters 98
   An Energetic Word 102
   The Borrowed Easter Egg 109
   Weed Seeds 119
   Lessons in Freezing 124
   The Christmas Star 133
   Alligator Removal Services 137
   No Rushing Allowed 149
   Neighborhood MVP 156
   Some Birthday! 163
   The River Run 167
   Lilacs 179

Appendices

   A. The Journey from a 'Telling Story' to a
      'Reading Story' and Back again 185
   B. Theological Foundations for the Stories 188
   C. Guide for Use of Cross-Over Stories that
      Work in Non-religious Settings 235
   Credits 265

Acknowledgements

I was a story-lover long before I was a storyteller. My mom and dad, Beverly and Bill Updegraff, made sure I was surrounded with stories throughout my childhood. Ministers and camp counselors, librarians and teachers (both public school and Sunday school), neighbors and friends, brothers Jon and Will as well as sister Julie, all sharing their stories with me as I grew could not know the critical role they were playing in the formation of a storyteller. When the Rev. Ernie Fowler of the First Congregational Church in Lodi, California called the children forward each Sunday to tell a story, I catapulted out of the pew ... it was a favorite part of my early church experience and one that I have incorporated into my own ministry.

For years, I used other people's stories for the 'Children's Message', but one Saturday night I could find nothing age-appropriate on the subject of forgiveness. In the dark hours after our sons had gone to bed, the *Alligator Removal Services* took shape in my mind. Bleary-eyed, but armed with a story for the Children's Message, I told of the rock that wasn't a rock at all, but an alligator egg ... well ... just read it. As I moved toward the exit with the children, my colleague walked past me and said quietly, "Publish it." He was the first of many to encourage me when I later began to collect the stories I'd 'made up'.

The Louisville Institute awarded me a sabbatical grant that allowed this project to begin in earnest. I attended a storytellers' workshop in Marblehead, Massachusetts with Judith Black and Doug Lipman as well as one of The Telling Place's workshops held at Hetton Hall, Chatton, Northumberland, UK under the leadership of Pam Potts. Each professional storyteller added to my own understanding and skill. Ultimately, thanks to the Louisville Institute's financial support, I was able to spend an entire month in Eastport, Maine, tucked away above *The Commons* in an apartment that looked across Passamaquoddy Bay to Campobello Island. The remarkable women who founded *The Commons* and provided so well for my stay include Meg McGarvey, Nancy Asante, Anna Baskerville, and especially Linda Godfrey. Thank you!

The never-ending encouragement of my church family at All Souls Church, especially the children over these many years, has made storytelling a joy and a challenge for me nearly every Sunday. There are a special few who must be singled out for their particular way of cheering me on. My colleague, Dr. James Haddix, a great storyteller in his own right, has helped me believe in the importance of this ministry. Nathaniel VerLee, a young man who has grown up knowing Uncle Sol, steadily gave me positive feedback as I initially captured these stories on paper. The Reverend AbbyLynn Campbell's enthusiastic support for the project helped keep me focused on why I have collected these stories. Then there is Dr. Carol Sherman, an encouraging friend, who not only donated a gazillion hours of time moonlighting as my unofficial editor, she also made the initial contact with the man who ultimately decided to publish this book. There are not enough gratitude words, Carol. Andrea Hand is both a great friend and a great artist. Her willingness to illustrate this book is sheer gift and a delight to my heart. A special thank you to Dr. David Trobisch from Quiet Waters Publications who invited both Andrea and me to enjoy an unhurried creative process even while trying to find a workable timetable.

Truth be told, without my family's sustaining love and care this book would not have happened. Spencer, Peter and Tyler have all listened to partially hatched stories and put up with an overly tired, grouchy, Sunday morning mom far more often than any of us cares to recall. Your antics have not only been a source of inspiration for the kids in Uncle Sol's neighborhood, you have been a constant source of inspiration in my life. I thank God for you! At the front of the line, before all others belongs my dear husband, Rex. You have been my strength, my greatest encourager and my most honest critic. I could never have lasted over these many years it has taken to reach this point without your never-failing love and support. I'm so grateful. And I am still incredulous at how God brought together a Mainer and a Californian!

Finally, the actual credit for all these stories belongs to Jesus, the Master Storyteller, who said, "That's why I tell stories: to create readiness, to nudge the people toward receptive insight." (Matthew 13:13a, The Message) He has been giving me stories to tell for years. It is a privilege and a blessing to share a small portion of them with you.

Renee U. Garrett
All Souls Church
Bangor, Maine
September 20, 2010

INTRODUCTION

"It may take a village in Africa to raise a child; but here in the United States of America, the equivalent is a good neighborhood." That was the thought that launched the creation of "Uncle Sol's neighborhood" as the setting for a series of stories about children of different ages with different family circumstances, growing up together on the street where Uncle Sol lives. These stories began as short 'children's messages' during the service of worship at All Souls Church, in Bangor, Maine where I serve as Minister of Christian Nurture. Over time, the characters have begun to take on lives of their own, especially Uncle Sol.

He has been identified by some listeners as a relative they once had and by others as a neighbor they know. The truth is Uncle Sol is a fictional character. However if one reads the Gospels, a light of recognition concerning his way of being in relationship with his neighbors should begin to flicker. Uncle Sol is beloved by young and old, men and women, parents and children alike. As a widower and an empty-nester, he's had his share of hardships, but he has become better rather than bitter. He is wise. He is not pushy. He is patient and kind. He is not arrogant or rude. He does not rejoice in the wrong, but rejoices in the right. He believes all things, hopes all things, and endures all things with every one of his neighbors in the neighborhood. He guides them in the paths of righteousness without them even knowing it.

Near the conclusion of C.S. Lewis's *The Lion, The Witch and the Wardrobe*, from the *Chronicles of Narnia*, Aslan enters the defeated White Witch's castle to bring life back to all those unfortunate creatures she had turned to stone. The lion moves from one stone statue to the next breathing on them.

With each breath from Aslan, the creatures come to life, all except one—the giant. A single breath of Aslan only makes the feet return to living flesh, but the great lion says, "If the feet are set right, the rest will follow." Uncle Sol breathes life into the neighborhood children through the kind of contact that helps 'set their feet right', assisting their growth toward the men and women God intended them to be from the moment they were formed in their mothers' wombs.

I have used a blend of fiction and actual experiences to communicate the reality of the power and presence of God in our daily lives. Many times I've been asked if a particular story is true. The answer I give is always this: "There is a lot of truth in the story." Some of the events within the stories do resemble experiences from my own childhood or from that of my sons while others have bubbled up from my imagination.

Please step into the neighborhood. Become part of a world that knows one of its garden-tending elder citizens happily shares the very breath of life that has filled his own. Perhaps you will discover ways to allow The Breath of Life to breathe life into your relationships within your own neighborhood. Perhaps God will use you to care for the roses which surround you right where you live. May the peace of our Lord Jesus Christ be with you!

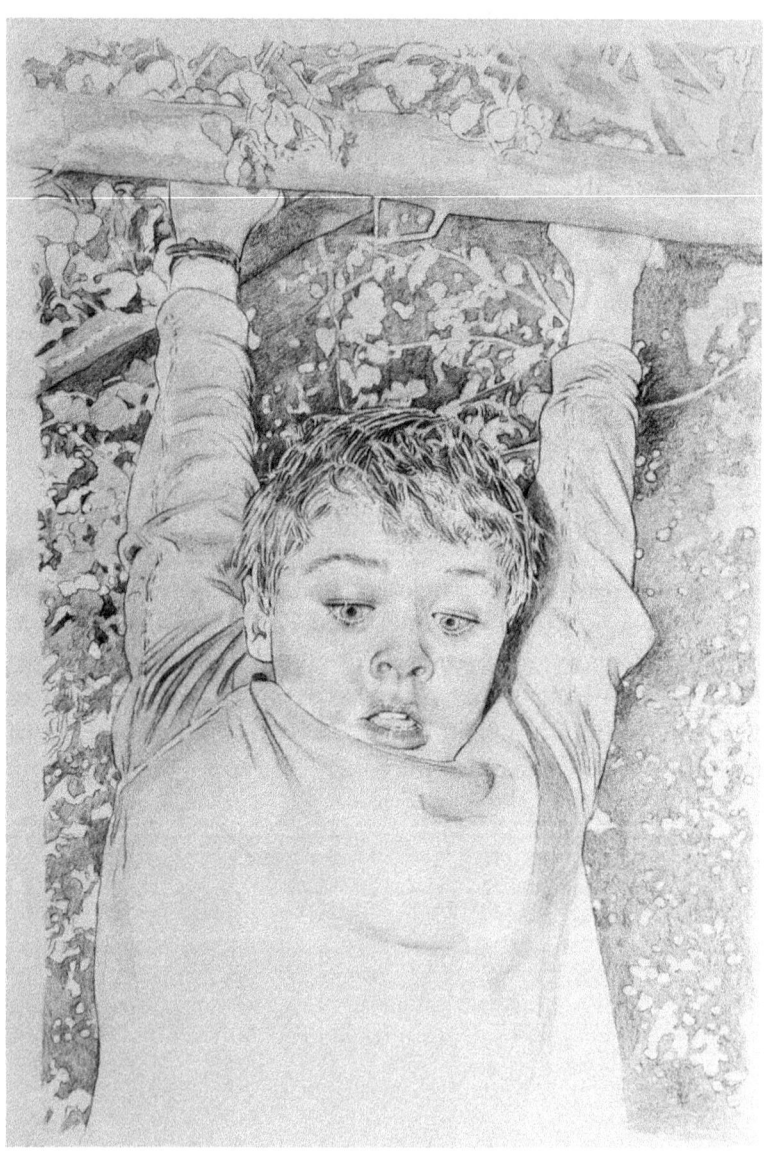

A Drop of Faith

It was the last tree. It always was. After all the other trees were trimmed and pruned, Uncle Sol finally reached this very last one at the far end of his huge garden. He saved it for last because it was his favorite tree and because it required the most care. The ancient chestnut tree was one of the few to have survived the awful disease that had wiped out most of the native chestnut trees in America. Every year Uncle Sol climbed up his tallest ladder to inspect the branches and trim away any strangely colored twigs. So far he had kept his tree alive. The chestnut was taller than all the others in Uncle Sol's garden, but it was hard to tell because the back of Uncle Sol's great yard sloped steeply away down the side of a hill where there was more rock than grass. Every time he inspected the tree he had difficulty finding a good place to put the ladder. This year was no different.

Uncle Sol carefully leaned the long extension ladder against the trunk about the same place he always did. But the moment he stepped on the first rung, the ladder began to wobble terribly. "The frost coming out of the ground this spring must have made it more uneven than last year," he thought to himself. He readjusted the ladder and stepped on the rung again. It was better, but still shaky. He decided to return to the garage to get some short pieces of wood to wedge under the legs of the ladder to make it more stable.

Unbeknownst to Uncle Sol, his young neighbor David had been watching the pruning and trimming from behind the bushes. David was one of the more adventuresome boys in the neighborhood. Sometimes he liked to pretend he was a secret agent, trying to discover information and he would hide behind bushes and crawl around on his stomach trying to get really close to people. Uncle Sol would just laugh whenever David popped up out of the bushes and he never scolded him, so David felt very comfortable playing his imaginary games in Uncle Sol's yard.

When he saw Uncle Sol leave the ladder unattended, David's first thought was to climb up into the tree and get into the branches to surprise Uncle Sol when he came back. He had always wanted to get into the chestnut tree, but the lowest branches were way too high for him to reach, no matter how hard he tried. When David stepped onto the first rung of the ladder, he felt it wobble, but he thought ... "I'll just climb it fast and it will be okay." David did climb fast ... but it wasn't "okay". The ladder started out wobbly, but the higher David got the more the ladder began to shake. Suddenly it began to swing sideways away from the tree. David was just able to grab hold of an overhanging branch as the ladder slipped away and clattered to the ground below. There he was, holding onto a branch high off the ground with a fallen ladder and rocks beneath him.

David didn't know what to do. He could barely see beneath his swinging feet, but there, directly below him, was the ladder draped over one of the larger rocks. "If I just let go and drop to the ground I'll break my leg or my arm or worse!" He looked above his head to the branch that was keeping him from certain disaster. There wasn't enough room to swing his leg up on it. He was too close to the trunk. And the trunk ... it was so large that he couldn't swing his legs around it either. He tried to move himself a little further away from the trunk to give himself more room to work, but the branch on the old chestnut was so much bigger than any of the other trees he was used to climbing, he felt like he was going to slip if he budged at all. That's when he decided to just start yelling, "Help! Help! Uncle Sol! Help me!"

Uncle Sol heard the panicked cry as he was emerging from the garage. He dropped the wooden wedges and began to run toward the backyard. As soon as he turned the corner around the end of the house, he could see that the ladder was no longer propped up against the tree. In its place he saw a pair of jeans and sneakers against the dark trunk, and although branches hid the rest of the body, he could easily guess who it was without seeing more. "Hold on, I'm coming!" Uncle Sol yelled as he hurried down the long grassy yard toward the hill. David was always lurking around and showing up in the strangest places. "There's only one child that could be," he said to himself as he hurried toward the chestnut tree. "Hang on! I'm nearly there, David."

David's hands were hurting. The rough bark was digging into his palms. His fingers were numb. His arms were hurting. He wasn't sure how long he could hold on. "Ohhhhh, my hands are slipping." As he tried to tighten his grip, he nearly slipped off the branch. Beads of sweat covered his forehead. He could feel his heart racing in his chest. Blood was pounding in his ears.

"Help, Uncle Sol, help me!" But his voice trailed away as he focused all his energy into holding onto the branch. "Uncle Sol isn't going to make it," he thought. "I'm going to fall." He closed his eyes and held on to the branch with what strength he had left.

Just then, he heard that familiar voice right below him.

"Don't let go, David! Just a minute … hang on. I'll help you …" Uncle Sol pulled the ladder out from under the tree. Positioning himself under David and a little behind him, he said, "David, I want you to do exactly what I tell you."

There was panic in David's voice. "Uncle Sol, Uncle Sol, … I, I can't see you, where are you?" " M'my hands are slipping! I'm gonna fall! I'm gonna get hurt."

There was calm in Uncle Sol's voice. "David, I won't let you get hurt, but you must do exactly as I tell you. I will catch you, but you have to let go of the branch and drop straight down. Don't twist around and don't kick." Even from behind the boy, Uncle Sol could see the struggle going on in David's mind as David clenched his jaw and tried to tighten his grip on the branch again, still swinging his legs in a useless attempt to wrap them around the trunk. "David, stop fighting and let yourself drop straight down."

All of a sudden, David grew still. His body relaxed. He let his hands slide off the branch and just let himself fall. And he fell right into Uncle Sol's waiting arms.

In the next moment, they were both sitting on the ground underneath the chestnut tree talking and laughing at the same time.

"Oh, Uncle Sol, I was so scared, I thought I was really gonna get hurt. I wasn't sure I could hold on till you got there and then I wasn't sure you could catch me ... but you did! You did!"

"David, you really frightened me! I knew I could catch you, but I was afraid you wouldn't believe that I could. If you hadn't trusted me to help you and done exactly what I said, you would really have gotten hurt."

"At first I didn't think you could do it because I couldn't see what you were doing, but then I thought, 'Uncle Sol has always done what he said he was going to do'. That's when I decided to relax and let go."

Uncle Sol unexpectedly turned serious, "Now promise me you won't ever climb up an unsteady ladder again ... ever. In fact, promise me that you won't climb up any ladder in my yard unless I'm right with you."

"Oh, I promise, Uncle Sol. Cross my heart and hope to die," said David as he made an X over his heart.

"No, *that* isn't necessary David, just a plain promise will do, thank you." Uncle Sol shook his head as he smiled and rolled his eyes toward the sky. "I think I'm going to get a drink of lemonade before I finish with that chestnut tree. Care to join me?"

The two neighbors walked back toward the house together, recounting to each other all over again the near accident and the great rescue. David could hardly wait to tell the other kids about Uncle Sol's great save. "You know, Uncle Sol, after my friends hear about this they're gonna want you to catch them, too! Maybe you'd better leave the ladder out!"

Uncle Sol just shook his head and laughed. "That's the best reason I've heard for putting it away, David."

1 Corinthians 15:20-26
Matthew 28

Theological Foundation: see p.188
Guide for Non-religious Settings: see p.235

Team Effort

Jenny loved to wear jewelry and everyone in the neighborhood knew she did. So when her birthday came each year, her friends would give her little necklaces or bracelets to wear. While Jenny was still a very little girl, her grandmother had brought her a watch necklace from Switzerland. The watch was made with gold and crystal. You could see 17 rubies in the gears of the watch by looking through the clear crystal backing. Jenny's mother let her wear whatever jewelry she wanted to wear to school except for the watch necklace—that was reserved for special occasions.

   Jenny had told many of her classmates about her watch with the 17 rubies. A number of the boys didn't believe you could see the rubies and began telling everyone that Jenny was making it up. That got Jenny really mad and she decided to prove she was telling the truth. The next day, Jenny did what she was not supposed to do: she wore the watch necklace to school. She hid it under her sweater on the way out of her house so her mother and father wouldn't see that she was taking the watch to school. Once she was on the bus, Jenny proudly pulled out the necklace from underneath the sweater. The beautiful watch impressed everyone, including the boys who had said she wasn't telling the truth. Through the clear crystal backing, the gears could be seen moving and the rubies sparkled as they held working parts together. After school was over that day, Jenny completely forgot she was wearing the watch necklace. She got off the bus and decided to play with friends instead of going home first.

   That's when it happened. A link in the necklace chain broke just as she was jumping over the storm drain, chasing after Jon. She felt it slip, but before she could grab it, the entire watch necklace slid between her fingers and down it fell through the grating over the storm drain. It was gone. Jenny dropped to her knees right on top of the storm drain and began to cry. It was really dark in that hole and she couldn't see her watch anywhere.

Uncle Sol was working in his garden and had noticed the children playing across the street. He saw Jenny drop to her knees and start to cry. By the time Uncle Sol got to her, several of the other children were already by her side giving her advice.

"Uncle Sol, I've lost my grandmother's watch necklace…" Jenny stammered between sobs. "I don't know what I'm going to do. I wasn't even supposed to be wearing it."

Uncle Sol was used to helping the children solve problems, but this one was going to be very difficult. He couldn't see anything when he looked through the bars on the storm grate. He tried to move it, but it was just too heavy.

"I need a flashlight," said Uncle Sol as he started to get up.

"Uncle Sol, I've got a flashlight right here!" It was Jon. He always had a flashlight in his pocket and extra batteries. Even when he got teased about it, he carried it around saying, 'You never know when you'll need light.' With Jon's flashlight Uncle Sol could see where the watch had landed. Inside the storm drain there was a piece of rock about 2 feet below the grate sticking out like a shelf. That ledge had saved the watch from falling all the way to the bottom of the drain. All the children peered down into the storm drain with Uncle Sol.

"Oh, that's crazy where it stopped! Usually there are straight sides right to the bottom!"

"How do *you* know? You always look into storm drains?"

"Yeah, as a matter of fact, I do. I like to see if any cool stuff is at the bottom."

"I think we should get a vacuum cleaner and suck it out."

"No way. That won't work. Nobody's got an extension cord that long. What we need is a big wad of gum on the end of a yardstick."

"Ahhhhhhh you're right ... I forgot about the extension cord. Gum? That's disgusting. Hey, ya know, we could..." Everybody was talking at the same time and offering ideas about how to get it out.

"Okay, everyone, quiet down," said Uncle Sol, trying to get a little order among all the competing ideas. "All of you have different ideas of how you'd get the watch out. How about each of you finds what you think will work and bring it back here?" While the others dashed off toward their homes, Jenny did not leave Uncle Sol's side. Within minutes, they were all back with the strangest assortment of things. Will brought a kite and David brought duct tape.

"I brought diaper pins, Uncle Sol. I'm sorry Helen is here, but Mom said I had to let her come with me. She's too little to help. I'll just try to keep her out of the way," Edie apologized.

Uncle Sol took Helen's hand and guided her to his side.

"Helen, you stay right next to me. I'm sure you'll be a help." Helen's face brightened considerably as she knelt down beside him. Then Uncle Sol looked at everyone's contribution and they could tell he was concentrating. "Hmmmm, I think this will work," he said with a smile. He took the long thin stick out of Will's kite and then he took a diaper pin from Edie. Next he used some of David's duct tape to attach the pin very tightly to the stick. "Now, Jon, hold the light so I can see where I'm headed."

Very slowly, very carefully Uncle Sol lowered the stick through the storm grate. The children were on their knees ringing the storm drain, heads peering into the hole, barely leaving enough room for Uncle Sol to maneuver the stick in just the right way.

"Give me just a little more room, Jenny," Uncle Sol said as she bumped his elbow trying to see better. "All right, don't move, anyone." With a twist of the stick Uncle Sol was able to use the open pin to catch the ring that held the watch on the necklace. As he slowly raised the stick up, nobody dared breathe ... especially Jenny.

Just as it was nearing the very top of the grating, Jenny cried out, "Uncle Sol, the chain is starting to slip off." Before the words were out of her mouth, a little hand had squeezed through the bars on the grating and reached out just in time to catch the chain as it slipped away from the watch. In the next moment, the watch was out and safely in Jenny's pocket along with the chain that little Helen had caught.

"Uncle Sol, you saved my life!" Jenny was so relieved.

"I didn't do that all by myself, Jenny. We all wanted to help you and each of us did in our own way."

"I had the flashlight!" said Jon as he waved it in the air. "I always have the flashlight!" They all laughed as each one waved his or her contribution in the air.

"I brought the kite with the handy stick," added Will.

"I brought the diaper pins with the extra long, sharp point," Edie said.

"And I brought the duct tape" said David with an air of finality.

"And Helen brought her hands," said Uncle Sol taking her tiny ones in his large ones for all to see. "All working together though, we did some fine rescue work, don't you think?" Jenny agreed and thanked every one of them.

While Jenny and her rescue crew sat on Uncle Sol's steps eating cookies and drinking milk, Uncle Sol said, "This rescue effort reminds me of an important lesson that I like to keep fresh in my mind."

"What's that, Uncle Sol?" Jon asked.

"Well, each person is special and each one of us is different. Sometimes we're able to solve problems and do things all by ourselves and it works out just fine. But…"

"But sometimes you try to do things by yourself and it doesn't work out at all," Will interrupted, attempting to finish Uncle Sol's statement.

Uncle Sol let Will finish and then added, "Ah, right. I *was* just going to take it a step further, Will. Today, we had a problem to solve and you each brought something to help solve the problem. Each thing by itself wouldn't have done us much good. Just a flashlight or just a pin, or just duct tape or just a stick or just our bare hands," Uncle Sol smiled over at Helen as he mentioned her important contribution, "would not have been enough to get that necklace out."

"Oh, I get it! I get it" Will jumped in again, "We each brought what we had and when we put it all together, we were able to solve the problem. And you're saying that's true for other people, too, aren't you?"

"That *is* what I'm thinking, Will," Uncle Sol replied. "Each of us has special gifts and talents and abilities that make all our lives better and certainly happier when we share them with others."

"Then I propose a toast," Will said as he raised his milk glass: "To sharing our special gifts and talents ... and our special stuff to help each other forever." Milk sloshed onto the steps as every glass came together.

"Oops, sorry Uncle Sol. I'll get a sponge," Will called out.

"I'll get some paper towels," Edie said.

"I'll get my dog," Jon said over all the rest.

Uncle Sol just shook his head and smiled.

1 Corinthians 12:4-11

Theological Foundation: see p.189
Guide for Non-religious Settings: see p.237

Kite Calamity

"Any of you ever make a kite before?" Uncle Sol asked the group of neighborhood children gathered around his picnic table after school one afternoon in early spring. They shook their heads, "no", as they looked around at each other. Not one of the children had ever made a homemade kite.

"I thought you could only buy kites. I didn't know you could make them," Julie said.

"Of course you can, if you have the right materials and a little instruction." Uncle Sol replied. "Kites are very simple to make. And Julie, there is nothing like sending a kite you made all by yourself way up into the sky. I'd be happy to teach any of you who would like to learn. Do I have any takers?" The instant loud chorus of "yeses" made Uncle Sol laugh.

Early on Saturday morning the kite-builders began to gather on Uncle Sol's deck. It was perfect kite flying weather—strong steady winds, warm and bright. Carefully laid out on the picnic table were the materials Uncle Sol had promised. String, paper, balsa wood sticks of two different lengths, wire, glue, a pile of fabric scraps and markers. When all the children had arrived, Uncle Sol explained how to make one.

"First you wire together the two sticks to make a cross shape. Next, you take the string and run a piece from one wooden end to the other around the outside of the cross so that it now looks like a diamond." After that Uncle Sol showed them how to cut out the right amount of paper in just the right shape for the kite, how to glue it around the string diamond and how to put a "bridle" on the kite so that a string could be attached to the front. The tail, made of fabric scraps, was the last part of the kite to be attached so that it would fly straight in strong winds.

"All right. That's all there is to it," said Uncle Sol as he finished his model. "There are enough supplies for everyone, so share and help each other … .and don't forget to decorate the paper for your kite before you glue it onto the string." The telephone started ringing and Uncle Sol left to answer it. "This is a long distance call I've been expecting from my brother. Julie, would you be sure everyone gets what they need?" he called over his shoulder.

Julie loved being put in charge of any group. She helped everyone wire his or her wood frames together and supervised the stringing and the gluing. Finally, she started her own kite. She was in such a rush to catch up with the other children that she not only used the wire to connect her two sticks, but she used the wire instead of string to connect all the ends of the sticks to form the diamond shape. She thought it was much faster because the wire wrapped so nicely around the ends and held tight. Once she had glued the paper over the diamond-shaped wire frame, it looked like all the other kites.

By the time Uncle Sol returned from the phone call, everyone was working on the tails for the kites. He helped with the finishing touches and then produced a special kite string on a spindle for each boy and girl. After Uncle Sol finished tying the string on Jon's and Will's kites, the two were ready to bolt, along with David, eager to test their kites in wind that had been building all morning.

"Listen up, everyone. Before you go anywhere, you need to know the rules. Kite flying is great fun, but you need to do it in safe places. Do *not* fly your kites near electric power lines or telephone wires or near trees. And don't fly your kite if you hear thunder. I don't want any of you repeating Ben Franklin's electricity experiment! Is that clear?"

"Yes!" they all shouted.

"I think your school yard is the best place to fly a kite because there are no trees and no power lines anywhere near it." Uncle Sol finished his lecture and waved 'good bye'.

The neighborhood kids left Uncle Sol's yard skipping, yelling and running, kites eagerly dancing on the ends of short strings following behind them.

"Aw, the school yard is so far from here, let's go to the field instead." Julie said, still assuming command of the little group.

"I don't know, there are a lot of trees right around the edge of the field," cautioned Jon.

"Yeah and the power lines are on the other side," added Will.

"It'll be all right. The wind is blowing right down the middle so our kites won't go near the trees or the power lines." Julie spoke so confidently that the other children followed her into the field. She was right, the wind was blowing right down the middle of the field and it didn't take long for the children to get their kites launched. The wind carried the eight kites so far up that they looked like tiny colored patches against the blue as they soared on their strings.

"My arm's getting tired holding the kite string," complained Will after a while, but before anyone could help him, the string escaped from his hand. A gust of wind burst past the children and yanked at all their kites, tearing the strings out of Jon's and David's hands, too. Up in the sky, a wild game of kite tag began when the escaping kites bumped into one kite and then another kite and another. The strings began to tangle and suddenly *all* the kites were tangled with each other. They were careening out of control and pulling so hard that the string was beginning to cut the fingers of the kite-flyers who were trying to reel theirs in. Julie struggled to hold on to the wildly spinning octopus of kites and tails. The children watched helplessly as the pile cart-wheeled toward the ground.

"Oh, no! Look!" yelled Jon. All eyes followed the clump of kites as it landed right on top of the power lines next to one of the transformers. There was a sizzling sound and then a bright blue light arching over the wires and a huge explosion. The paper kites burst into flames. The kids watched in disbelief and shock as the ball of flaming kites fell from the power lines and landed in the tall grass underneath.

"I told you we should go to the school like Uncle Sol said!" Jon groaned.

"We are in so much trouble," added Will.

"It's your fault, Julie, you said it would be all right." accused David.

The other kids joined David, "It's all your fault, Julie. You told us it was okay…"

That's when they heard the fire engines in the distance. They looked at each other. "This is bad, Julie. This is really bad. You are in so much trouble." David clearly wanted no part of taking the blame for this, even though his kite was burning with all the rest. And, without a word being said, they all bolted for home.

When Julie arrived at her house, she discovered, like all the other kite-flyers, that there was no electrical power anywhere in the neighborhood.

"Hi Mom, I'm home." Julie called out as she rushed for the stairs up to her bedroom.

"Oh, Julie, wait. We don't have any power. I don't know what happened," Julie's mother called out to her. Julie froze midway up the stairs, "It's odd to lose power on a day it isn't storming and the wind isn't wild." Her mother continued, "Maybe a tree branch fell on the lines or something. I hope there wasn't a car accident."

Julie suddenly felt cold and her hands felt sweaty. She could feel her heart speed up as her mother continued to talk. "You know, Julie, we got a newsletter from the power company last week that said any repairs needed on power lines would be charged to the families in the neighborhood if it was actually somebody's fault instead of an accident of nature like a tree falling or an ice storm. That's why I hope it's a tree or something like that. I suspect it's pretty expensive to have the power restored."

"I'm going to my room, I've got some stuff to do." Julie said as she tried to get away before the tears began to slide from the corners of her eyes. From her bedroom window she could see the line crews already working on the power lines and a firefighter holding up pieces of charred rags and twisted wire. Then she saw three familiar forms walking in the field toward her house. David, Jon and Will came through the backyard gate and called up to her window.

"Hey, Julie, you better come down."

Julie scurried down the stairs and quietly slipped out the front door away from the kitchen where her mother was working

"What are you talking about?" Julie asked after she had dragged the three boys out toward the street.

"The firefighters asked if we knew who had been flying kites made of wire so we told them it was you and then they asked where you lived and we told them and they're on their way over here."

No sooner had the boys finished reporting the conversation than the low rumble of a large truck engine changing gears filled the street. There was the fire engine and it was slowing down right in front of Julie's house.

"Are you the girl who made the wire kite?" the firefighter asked as he stepped down from the vehicle. There was no smile on this firefighter's face like there had been when they had come to school to talk about fire safety. Back then, Julie had thought all the firefighters were friendly people wanting to help save lives, but now she was not so sure.

"Do you have any idea how dangerous this kite is?" the firefighter asked as he dangled the mangled wire in front of the children. "Not only did this kite connect the power wires and blow out the power to the whole neighborhood, but when they all fell to the ground burning, they caught the dry grass on fire underneath it. You'll see the burned area by the power pole. It could have spread to some of these houses near the field."

By this time Julie, Jon, Will and David were not alone. Julie's mom had come outside, too, and the rest of the neighborhood kids had appeared, but stood at a distance. Many of the other neighbors came out to hear what had happened. Worst of all, there was Uncle Sol listening to the firefighter ask,

"Were you at the school when we gave our program on fire safety?" Julie nodded, but she was afraid to talk for fear of bursting into tears. "Do you remember what we said about power lines and kites?" Julie nodded again, fully aware that Uncle Sol had told them all the same thing just before they'd left to fly their kites.

Suddenly Julie found her voice, "The rest of the kids flew their kites, too. It wasn't just me. We all did and if Will hadn't let go of his kite none of this would have happened." She wasn't willing to take all this blame herself. Out of the corner of her eye though, she could see how disappointed Uncle Sol looked.

"Well, you'll have to work that out with the power company because they are going to charge whoever's involved with the cost of the repair. But right now, since you're the girl with the wire kite, you are responsible." The firefighter stepped over to talk with Julie's mother while the boys quietly slipped away.

Later that day, Julie let all the others know how angry she was with them for having hidden and allowing her to take all the blame for "the Kite Disaster," as everyone was calling it. "I mean we were all together in this. Any one of you could have said, 'No Julie, it's too dangerous' and refused to fly your kites and gone to the schoolyard yourselves, but none of you did. You all joined right in and we were all having a good time. I mean, Will, it's just as much your fault as it is mine."

"I know. Uncle Sol said that every one of us disobeyed the rules that we'd been told twice—once at school and then again when he sent us off from his house with our kites. I think he's sorry he ever showed us how to make kites. He didn't say that, but he just looked really sad and disappointed in us," Will concluded.

When word came of the cost of the power-line repair, it was really bad news. Her parents had already decided that

Julie was going to have to earn the money to pay for the repair even before they saw how much it was.

"Disobedience has a high cost—sometimes a very high cost and you may as well learn that now," they had told her after listening to the whole story of how her wire kite got caught up in the power lines.

Julie had no idea how she could earn enough money to pay for the repair. It was more money than she had ever seen in her whole life, let alone earned. She'd be out of high school before her weekly allowance would pay for it. She was certain of that. Her babysitting jobs wouldn't help much at all. She had no hope of her parents backing down. They insisted that she figure out how to earn the money. No matter how Julie added up the numbers, she was sure she was going to be penniless forever. Still, she knew she was the cause of the trouble and she was determined to repay her parents for the cost of the repairs to the electric lines.

She began doing small jobs for the neighbors, but she carefully avoided Uncle Sol. She hadn't talked to him since the day of the power outage. That's why she was surprised when she got home from school one afternoon to find a note on her bed.

"Uncle Sol would like some help in his garden when you get home from school today," it read. Julie changed from her school clothes into her shorts. She could barely bring herself to climb the front steps of his house to ring the doorbell. When the door opened, Julie stammered,

"Uncle Sol, I'm so sorry for not listening to you … I mean you told us not to fly the kites near the power lines. I know you were counting on me and I blew it." Tears trickled down Julie's cheeks. Uncle Sol just listened while she went on to explain how she had to pay for the repair and that it was going to take forever and that she understood why her parents were making her earn the money, but that she was so discouraged because even working for neighbors after school every day had barely made a dent in what she owed her parents.

"I know, Julie. The other neighborhood kids have told me that you can't play after school anymore. I've watched you working for the other neighbors for weeks now. That's why I thought I would hire you to help me weed the yard."

Julie worked beside Uncle Sol the rest of the afternoon until suppertime. As she was washing her hands in Uncle Sol's kitchen sink, he wrote out a check for her work.

"Here Julie, thank you for the help," Uncle Sol said as he handed it to her. Julie took it and glanced at it as she was started for the door. She stopped still. It was the exact amount she had left to pay on the repair.

"Uncle Sol, I can't take this. I don't deserve it ... I didn't earn it ... I mean you can't give that much money to me. I'm supposed to earn it all myself."

Uncle Sol just smiled. "Well, it is up to you whether or not you take it, Julie. I can't force you to, of course. And you're right; you don't deserve it for the three hours of weeding you've done. But I can pay you what I want. That's *my* choice."

"My parents will never let me accept this."

"I've already had a very long conversation with your mother and father about what I was planning and they're okay with it now. They're satisfied that you've realized the serious consequences of disobeying safety rules."

"Oh, I have, Uncle Sol, I really have." Only then did the wrinkles in Julie's forehead begin to smooth away and for the first time in weeks, the glimmer of a smile appeared. "You mean that my parents will let me accept this and use it to finish paying them back and then I won't owe them anything more?"

"Well, not at least for the power line repairs, you won't," he said with a twinkle in his eye.

The tentative smile gave way to a full ear-to-ear grin. "You mean I'm free? I can play after school again? I can stop worrying about where I'll find another job to help me earn the money?"

As the reality of Uncle Sol's gift sank in, Julie began to jump up and down and she gave Uncle Sol a big hug.

"Thank you, Uncle Sol, thank you! Thank you! You've set me free. I'm free, I'm free!" She hugged him again and then leaped down the stairs. "I can hardly wait to tell everyone I can play again." With that Julie began skipping, bouncing and dancing all the way home.

Genesis 3:1-7
Romans 5: 12-19

Theological Foundation: see p.191
Guide for Non-religious Settings: see p.238

Lemonade Wisdom

"So, Edie, you want to grow beans this year?" Uncle Sol said. The elder neighbor was leaning on the rake he'd just been using to clear out some of last fall's leaves from underneath the bushes in his front yard when Edie, his twelve year old neighbor stopped by. Edie loved to grow plants in addition to all the other things she loved to do. She was very good at nearly everything she tried, but all the children in the neighborhood knew that Edie was also a bit of "a know it all." Nobody could tell Edie anything because she always knew more than anybody, at least that's what she liked everyone to believe.

"Everyone knows you're the best gardener in the whole neighborhood, Uncle Sol, so this year I want you to teach me how to grow green beans."

"Well, first you need to make sure…" Uncle Sol started, but Edie cut him off.

"I know, I know, I have to make sure that I find a nice sunny place for the beans to grow."

"Right, Edie. Then, it's important to break up the soil," Uncle Sol tried to continue.

"Oh! Oh! I know, so that the roots can push down and the sprouts can push up."

"That's right. Then…"

"Then I mark out the rows like it says on the package, and I plant the seeds about one half inch deep."

"Well, not exactly, but once you've done that, Edie…"

"Well, once I've done *that*, I have to make sure that I keep them watered, and use fertilizer to make sure they get everything they need."

"Sounds like you don't really need any help, Edie." Uncle Sol looked away past the girl and up at the leaves in the trees which were waving at him as the warm spring breeze through them.

"Well, Uncle Sol, I came over because I know you must have some special tips for growing beans. I mean the rest of your plants always look so good. So what else do I need to know?"

Uncle Sol looked as though he'd made up his mind about something when he turned back to his young neighbor and said, "Edie, why don't we go out on the deck and have some lemonade to drink while we discuss my special tips on growing beans?"

Uncle Sol led Edie to the picnic table on his deck. He motioned to her to sit down while he went inside his house. In just a couple of minutes he was back with a pitcher of lemonade and two glasses.

"Here you go, Edie," Uncle Sol said as he began to fill her glass.

Edie watched as Uncle Sol carefully filled the glass. As it got nearer to the top she expected Uncle Sol to slow down, but he didn't. He kept right on pouring. Edie wondered if Uncle Sol's eyesight was getting bad because he just kept pouring the lemonade. First it spilled over the side of the glass, then it made a big puddle on the table and then it formed a little stream and flowed off the table and onto the deck.

"Uncle Sol, stop! What are you doing?!" Edie cried out as she jumped up. "The glass is already full!"

"I'm just pouring lemonade into your glass, Edie," he answered innocently as he leveled off the pitcher.

"But Uncle Sol, you kept pouring and it went right over the top and spilled all over the table."

Uncle Sol put the pitcher of lemonade down. Looking steadily into Edie's face he said, "Edie, I was trying to teach you something about growing beans."

"What?" asked the very puzzled young neighbor.

"I was pouring the lemonade into your glass to teach you something about growing beans," Uncle Sol repeated. "You see, you asked me to teach you about beans, Edie. But every time I tried to tell you something more about beans, you told me what you already knew instead. You're just like the full glass of lemonade. I tried to give you some of my knowledge and some of what I've learned from experience, but there wasn't any room."

Edie was quiet for a moment, "Oh, Uncle Sol, my mother says I do that all the time. I mean I guess I'm not really listening, I'm just thinking about what I know. I guess I *am* kind of full of myself."

"Well, let's just say that there isn't much room for new information," the elder neighbor's eyes twinkled as he smiled at the girl across the table.

"All right, Uncle Sol, let's try again. I am listening this time."

"And I'm pouring," Uncle Sol said as he filled the second glass of lemonade and then wiped up the mess with paper towels he'd hidden in his pocket. "Now about those beans…"

Matthew 13: 13-17

Theological Foundation: see p.193
Guide for Non-religious Settings: see p.239

Inner Change

Alice had visited Uncle Sol's neighborhood every summer for as long as any of the children could remember. Alice's Aunt Barbara lived beside the lake at the far end of the neighborhood and each year Alice, along with all her cousins, would come to visit when summer was at its brightest and the weather turned hot. Alice seemed to be the quietest of all Mrs. Hodge's nieces and nephews, rarely speaking to any of the neighborhood kids who gathered to swim at the lake. But now that Alice and her mother had moved in for good, the children became aware of just how quiet she really was.

Although Alice seldom spoke in class and never on the bus, two things about her were clear to everyone. Alice loved books—she was always reading and spending time at the library—and Alice was sad.

"I don't think I've ever heard Alice laugh since she moved here, have you?" Jenny asked one Saturday after she watched Alice walk up her front steps with the mail from the mailbox.

"I sure haven't. I don't even think I've seen her smile," David added. Julie and Jon, two of the neighborhood children, were certain that they had overheard their parents talking one day about Alice's family. "Well, I guess Alice's father and brother and the whole family was out for a ride one day and some drunk driver hit them. Right in the middle of the day, can you believe it? Well, Alice's father and brother were killed, and Alice was hurt pretty badly, too. That all happened when Alice was little. Ever since then Alice and her mom have moved around a lot and now they've moved in with Alice's aunt. Mom said Alice and her mom not only lost half their family, they lost any place to really call home."

"That's awful," Jenny said shaking her head.

"I can't imagine losing my father and a brother and my home," David agreed and went on to say, "That kinda explains everything, doesn't it? I mean no wonder Alice is so sad all the time."

"No wonder she's reading all the time! It must help her take her mind off things…" Jenny shook her head trying to get rid of the thought that had just crept in, 'what if that had been my family …?'

There was no sudden change in the way any of the four treated Alice. They didn't want to intrude on her silent sadness and they felt very awkward, not knowing what to really say to her now that they knew her story.

One day Alice was walking home from the library when she stopped to look at the beautiful flowers in Uncle Sol's yard. He had the brightest yard in the whole neighborhood. No matter what part of the growing season it was, Uncle Sol's flower garden was blooming. It was a matter of general knowledge around the neighborhood that anyone was welcome to wander in his yard to look at the flowers so long as they treated his property with respect. The neighborhood kids were particularly welcomed so long as they were careful and didn't play ball near the flowers. While Alice may not have talked much, she listened a lot and she had heard about the open invitation into Uncle Sol's yard. She had grown accustomed to taking quiet walks among the flowers when no other kids were around. She was so lost in thought as she stopped in front of a patch of day lilies that she never even saw Uncle Sol weeding around some bushes near the corner of the house

"Hi, Alice, aren't they beautiful this time of day? I love the way the afternoon sun makes their colors even brighter," Uncle Sol said as he stood up to stretch.

Alice nearly jumped straight up in the air and managed to drop her books all over the grass, she was so startled.

She immediately bent down to pick up her books and then said quietly, "The flowers are really beautiful." Uncle Sol smiled. That might have been the end of the conversation as

Alice turned to go, but Uncle Sol wasn't the kind of a grown-up who would just let a child pass through his yard without a little conversation.

"I understand from your mother that you are quite a reader. What books did you get from the library this time?

"The same kinds of stories I always read. I like stories where the girl or the boy uncovers a mystery about themselves ... something he or she never knew and then it changes their whole life for the better." Pointing to the book on top, she added, "This is my absolute favorite—where the girl is raised on a poor little farm far from other people. The family tells her that she is not their child and she doesn't know who her real family is, but she's determined to find out. She has to search and search and goes through all kinds of danger, but then she comes upon a beautiful city that is ruled by a very kind king. After an accidental encounter with the king, she discovers that she is the long lost daughter who was kidnapped by the king's enemies and given up for dead. She is welcomed into the palace as the princess and the nicest king in all the world is her real father."

"Sounds like you know that story by heart," Uncle Sol commented, noticing how her face brightened as she told it to him. It was obvious that the story was very important to her.

Alice looked down at the lawn as she admitted, "I *have* borrowed it from the library a few times." As soon as she finished there was a long pause and the girl began to move toward the garden gate. Uncle Sol weighed his next words before saying, just as she reached the gate,

"Sounds like you, Alice."

"What do you mean?" Alice asked.

"I mean, it sounds like you. That could be your story."

"Uncle Sol, don't you know I don't have a father anymore? I'll never have a father like the princess in that story."

"Alice, I do know your father died along with your brother. I've actually had a number of conversations with your mother." Uncle Sol was very gentle with his words.

"I know that all the wishing and all the praying in the world can't change what's happened in your life. I know your heart and your mother's heart will always carry some sadness. Even so, there's an important way in which you *are* like the princess in the story."

Alice had been looking at her feet, but she looked over sideways at Uncle Sol with a very puzzled look on her face.

"I see you in church nearly every Sunday with your mother, so I know you know who Jesus is…"

Alice nodded and said, "Jesus Christ is God's son, our Savior."

"That's right. Do you know that Jesus said that when anyone welcomes him and believes him, he makes that person a child of God?

"I've heard that before…"

"Do you know what that really means, then?"

Alice shook her head "no".

"You've been adopted into God's family. You are Jesus' sister … that means, Alice, that you are God's daughter. Jesus' father is your father." Uncle Sol stopped to let that sink in. A flicker of understanding crossed Alice's face as she began to let her mind imagine this possibility.

"God is in heaven, but don't let that fool you, Alice. He is very, very close to you … closer than your own breath. He watches over you day and night and knows just what you're feeling, even how much your heart aches at times. He loves you very much."

Alice started to speak and then stopped herself.

"Yes, Alice?"

Alice looked even shyer than usual, but she finally put words to the thoughts that had been swirling around in her head, "Well, it's just, kinda hard to remember all that. I mean for a minute I could imagine it. Really, I could almost see God welcoming me into the great palace and telling everyone, 'This is my long-lost daughter, Alice. She's home.'"

"*I* can certainly imagine it, Alice … because it just happens to be true. You can talk to him anytime you like, you know;

he'll always listen. He cares deeply about you. He'll always be with you, no matter where you go in life. He just needs you to pay attention to him, that's all." Uncle Sol started to chuckle and Alice looked at him with an expression that asked, "What's so funny?" "Well, Alice, I think I am going to have to bow and begin to call you 'Your Highness' whenever you pass by."

"Why would you do that?"

"God is the King of the Universe and you are his daughter so that must mean you are a ... princess."

"Oh Uncle Sol ... you're silly." But even as Alice said that, she felt something inside her change and Uncle Sol could actually see it on her face. She was realizing something she hadn't even imagined moments before, and just thinking about it made her smile. The smile bubbled up from somewhere deep within her heart. For the first time since moving into her aunt's home, Alice's eyes sparkled. This was a whole new understanding of things ... she was special ... very special indeed. She was a beloved daughter of a heavenly Father who would always be near. For just a moment, Uncle Sol was quite sure he saw Princess Alice as she walked out of his yard through the garden gate.

Mark 9:2-13

Theological Foundation: see p.195

A New Home for Christmas

When Nick first moved into the neighborhood, he really didn't know anyone at all. He'd left his old school, his old friends ... *everything* and he felt lonely ... *really* lonely because it was Christmas time. Moving into a new town when there was only a week before Christmas meant that he'd probably get left out of any holiday celebrations in his new school. And he was right—because no one expected him.

He walked around the neighborhood looking at the houses where he had figured out kids lived. He saw their Christmas trees and colored lights. And he looked at his own house: boxes. That was all. Stacks and stacks of unopened boxes. His mother said they would get a Christmas tree if she could find the decorations amid all the packing boxes, but that didn't seem very likely to him. He was so lost in thought about how rotten his Christmas was going to be this year that he didn't even hear the old man say, "Hello" the *first* time. When Uncle Sol spoke a second time, Nick looked up.

"Oh, hello."

"You're new here. You're Nick, aren't you?"

"Yeah. How'd you'd know?"

"Oh, I've got my ways."

When Nick looked a bit worried, Uncle Sol laughed and said, "I've got a lot of friends in the neighborhood. They keep me pretty well informed of who's moving in. Lookin' forward to Christmas?"

Nick knew the right answer was supposed to be an enthusiastic "Yes", but he just nodded. He managed to say, "Good bye." Then he kept on walking. He was feeling much too sorry for himself to be around anyone friendly.

When he got home, his mother said that one of the neighborhood children had dropped off a bag of candy spearmint leaves. Nick looked at the bag. It had been tampered with: red duct tape closed an obvious cut in the bag and inside was a folded piece of paper.

Carefully peeling back the tape, Nick pulled out the paper and found that it was a story written in colorful red and green crayons. The story was about an orphaned boy who had been taken to an orphanage right around Christmas. The other children told him that on Christmas Eve they all got an orange. This was very special because during the rest of the year, they got nothing like that at all.

That was it. The story stopped mid-sentence. There wasn't anything else. Nick thought that was strange and he threw the unfinished story on his bedside table.

On the last day of school in the last class before Christmas break, a bag of M&Ms appeared on Nick's desk. When he moved the bag, a folded piece of paper with rather scrawly handwriting fell to the floor. Nick opened the note and read, "The orphan boy was pretty excited as Christmas day approached. On Christmas Eve there was a huge party—wonderful food and sure enough, the children were asked to line up so that they could receive their oranges. The new orphan boy stood expectantly at the end of the line, but as he stepped up to the director of the orphanage, the fellow looked very sad. The director told the boy that he was sorry, but that there was no orange for the new resident because when the order for oranges had been placed, the boy had not yet come. The orphan turned and ran from the room and threw himself down on his bed." That's where the story stopped...

"That's awful," thought Nick, "and that's how I've been feeling. Like nobody cares. I'm so left out in this new place." Still he couldn't help but look at the faces of his classmates, wondering who'd left the candy ... who might be making an attempt to be friendly.

Then, on Christmas Eve morning, Nick's father came into his room. Nick was arranging his car collection on the book shelves when a bag of pretzels was held out before his eyes with the familiar red duct tape on it.

"Dad, did you see who brought this?"

"One of the kids in the neighborhood, wouldn't come in and she wouldn't leave her name. Pretzels ... an odd Christmas gift, don't you think?"

Nick nodded as he took the bag. He immediately pulled off the folded piece of construction paper taped to the side of the bag and read words that had been cut out of magazines and glued on the page: "The orphan boy cried himself to sleep. He had no idea how long he slept, but he was awakened by a knock at the door. When he opened it, there stood one of the little girl orphans with a shy smile on her face. In her hands was a whole orange made up of many orange segments. She gestured for the boy to take the Christmas treat. It seems the other orphans had each donated a part of their orange so he could have a whole one. As he slowly took the orange from her hands, he thought, 'Maybe this will be a place I can call home'. His whole life began to improve from that moment on."

"Lucky him," thought Nick. Then he noticed another slip of paper taped to the bag. "Come get the pieces to your new home at the house with the star on the chimney," it read. "P.S. If you haven't eaten all the candy and pretzels yet, bring those, too."

Nick thought for a moment, "House with a star ... house with a star ... oh, yeah, that's the house where the old man lives."

He wasn't sure what to expect, but his curiosity got the best of him. Since he had nothing better to do the rest of the morning, he hiked up the street, stepped up to the door and knocked. Uncle Sol opened the door. "I've been expecting you, Nick. Come in." Only when he stepped inside did he see many of the other kids from the neighborhood, giggling and telling each other to be quiet.

"Welcome, Nick! Welcome to the neighborhood! Merry Christmas!"

Nick just stood there, frozen. Uncle Sol took the bag that held the candy and pretzels from his hand. That's when Jon stepped forward and handed Nick a piece of a gingerbread cookie that was shaped like the side of a house. Then Will did the same thing and so did Jenny and Edie and then Alice gave him two roof pieces … .until Nick's hands were full of gingerbread cookie pieces.

Nick didn't know what to say, he just stood there in the circle of children, hands cradling all the pieces, trying not to drop anything.

"Now, Nick there is not much you can do with all these pieces," began Uncle Sol.

"Well, he could just sit down and eat them," laughed Edie.

"Or he could turn them into a real gingerbread house like we planned," Uncle Sol answered back.

"Okay, Uncle Sol. I've got the tube of frosting all ready to go," Julie called from the kitchen.

"Right this way, Nick." Uncle Sol guided the still stunned Nick into the kitchen area that was really a wide open kitchen/dining room/family hanging-out space. Julie pulled out a foil-covered board and motioned Nick to put his pieces down on the table.

"I thought if you had a little help building this gingerbread house, you'd be able to take it home and enjoy it Christmas morning, Nick." Uncle Sol smiled as he continued. "I've helped nearly everyone here make a gingerbread house at one time or another."

"Oh, remember Uncle Sol, when we made mine? I put chocolate chips and cinnamon dots all over it. When I think of it now, it was pretty ugly; but at the time, I thought it was the most beautiful house I'd ever seen. I kept it for months and wouldn't let anybody touch it." Jenny shook her head and rolled her eyes at the memory. "Nick, I'm sure you'll make yours look way better than I did. I was pretty little when I did mine," Jenny added.

"And mine? Uncle Sol, remember how I used pretzels to build fences and all I wanted to do was build fences? You kept trying to get me to actually put the house together without actually telling me I had to." David popped a pretzel in his mouth just for proper emphasis.

Conversations swirled around Nick as he tried to follow Edie's guidance on how to handle the frosting tube. Uncle Sol held one side of the house in place and Will held the other side while the frosting hardened. There were so many hands helping that Nick had trouble keeping faces and fingers connected, but there was a lot of laughter and fun. Nick found himself telling everyone about his old neighborhood and some of his old friends and answering all kinds of questions about his favorite games, movies, school subjects and more.

Before long the cookie pieces were transformed into a gingerbread house with candy shutters and a sugar wreath right on the door. David helped make the pretzel fence that surrounded the whole house and just for good measure Jenny suggested that Nick put chocolate chips across the top of the roof. The gingerbread house was perfect with the fancy white frosting decorations around windows, door and gables. Nick surveyed the finished project and said, "This looks so good I want to eat every bit of it up right now and … I never want to touch it! I want to keep it forever!"

Julie chuckled, "That's what we've all said when we finished. I kept mine for about a month and then … I ate it!"

"Me, too."

"Yeah, me, too!" One after another of the children confessed to falling away from the resolve to 'save the gingerbread house 'forever'.'

"Well, Nick, we have one more thing to give you," Uncle Sol called from the family room side of the kitchen. "Come on over here and open it. This is so you can find us when you need us." Nick took one last look at his masterpiece and walked over to where Uncle Sol was holding out a wrapped package for him. Inside was a homemade book with a picture of each of the neighborhood kids, their phone numbers, and a map marking the exact house on the street where they lived. Nick didn't know what to say. It seemed clear everyone was inviting him to come over after Christmas. His head was spinning.

And that lonely, this-is-going-to-be-the-worst-Christmas-ever feeling he'd had when he knocked on the door? That disappeared somewhere between the gingerbread cookie pieces being placed into his hands and the pages of Nick's new phone book. He looked up at Uncle Sol, trying to find the words to say, "thank you", but Uncle Sol's smile told Nick, without any words at all, that he already knew. As Nick walked home carrying the gingerbread house, he found himself thinking, "Maybe this will be a place I can call home." And his whole life began to improve from that moment on.

Galatians 3:26-29
John 1: 10-13

Theological Foundation: see p.196

An Unexpected Flower

Uncle Sol loved his garden. He especially loved the flowers that bloomed in spring because he thought people needed to see the bright colors of crocuses and tulips and daffodils after a long winter. Once he retired, he devoted hours and hours of time to the gardens around his house. He planted bright flowers all over his garden so that everywhere you turned, spring, summer or fall, there was color. The kids of the neighborhood all loved to play in Uncle Sol's huge back yard because he had a jungle gym, sandbox and swing set everyone could use. And beyond all the playground equipment, there was still room for the older kids to play a game of soccer or football or wiffle ball if they were careful. All the neighborhood children loved the flowers and they loved the freedom to come and play in Uncle Sol's yard. And they all knew they were welcome as long as they followed Uncle Sol's rules.

One spring, flowers were already blooming when a new boy, Rocky, moved to the neighborhood.

"Hey Uncle Sol, have you met Rocky, the new kid that's moved in with his grandparents?" Jon asked as he helped the older neighbor ready the window boxes for planting.

"I can't say as I have, Jon. I did see a boy I didn't recognize the other day and when I waved he just looked away."

"That's him," Jon sighed. "It's like he's wearing a big 'Do Not Disturb' sign around his neck."

"Well, the boy I saw looked a bit older than most of you fellas."

"Oh, that's him, Uncle Sol. He's a year ahead of Nick in school."

"We've all given up trying to be friendly. It's no use."

"Jon, don't be so quick to give up on people. Some just take longer to convince that we're eager to welcome them into the neighborhood."

"Don't hold your breath on this kid, Uncle Sol," Jon concluded. Then changing subjects completely, "I was wondering if you're still going to hold the neighborhood 'Biggest Watermelon' contest this year. I've been reading about how to get them to be monster sizes."

The next day after school, Rocky was walking down the street toward his home when he stopped in front of Uncle Sol's house. He'd heard the kids on the bus talk about this older neighbor who welcomed anyone of the neighborhood families into his yard and he'd seen the kids playing over there all the time. The gate was open and none of the other kids were around yet. Rocky unconsciously shrugged his shoulders and stepped through the gate. He looked at all the carefully tended beds of spring flowers and then began to follow the path around the house to the backyard. Uncle Sol was in the middle of putting new potting soil in the window boxes when he heard the crunch of footsteps on the gravel path. Looking up, he was surprised to see the new boy.

"Hi there, my name's Sol Goodwens, but everyone just calls me Uncle Sol." Uncle Sol was wiping the dirt off his hands as he stepped toward the new boy, reaching out to offer a handshake, but Rocky just turned on his heel and left without saying a word.

From then on, Uncle Sol began to watch for Rocky, nodding his head ever so slightly as he smiled to let the new neighbor know he was noticed. If Uncle Sol caught Rocky's eye as he walked to or from the bus stop, Uncle Sol would smile and say, "Hi." If Rocky acknowledged the older neighbor at all, it was with a scowl. "This one's going to be tough to win over," Uncle Sol thought to himself every single time Rocky turned away.

Each spring Uncle Sol left the neighborhood to visit one of his grown-up children for a week. And each year while he was away, he left the gate to his yard unlocked so that the children could still play after school. It had never been a problem since neighborhood parents took turns being out in the backyard to supervise the smaller children in the afternoons. But this year, while Uncle Sol was away, there was a problem and it didn't happen in the afternoon.

"Oh my gosh, look!" Jenny exclaimed, pointing at Uncle Sol's house as the children gathered to catch the morning school bus. The children ran from the bus stop over to the picket fence separating Uncle Sol's yard from the sidewalk.

"Oh, no! What happened?"

"Who did this?"

"It wasn't like that when we left yesterday. It's terrible."

"Oh poor Uncle Sol, all those flowers."

"Yeah, all the time he spends out here."

"Uncle Sol's coming home in three days. What a rotten thing to come home to."

Flowers were thrown all over the lawn. Everywhere, daffodils and tulips lay broken and wilting on the grass. There were big holes in the flowerbeds where the bulbs had been pulled up. Some bulbs were lying in the street with their mangled flowers still attached. It was awful. Some of the younger kids began to cry when they saw Uncle Sol's ruined garden. The gate was standing wide open, so Jon just quietly walked over to it, removed a wilted tulip dangling from the latch and closed the gate. That afternoon, many of the kids and some of the parents began cleaning up the mess. They piled everything in a wheelbarrow and left it out back by the deck under the cover of a tarp. "I guess that's all we can do until Uncle Sol comes home," Jon and Julie's mother said as they finished sweeping the dirt off the sidewalk and driveway. The kids found other yards to play in since it just didn't feel right to go on using his yard as if nothing had happened. Even in each other's yards the somber feelings left in the wake of the vandalism to their special neighbor's property did not go away.

It wasn't long after Uncle Sol's return that the story of what actually happened to his flowers came out. The kids all huddled around Jon to hear it as they waited for the morning bus.

"Well, my mother talked to Uncle Sol and he told her that the police were doing their usual neighborhood check ... you know, when they drive through just to look around and make sure everything is okay ... and that's when they saw flowers flying across the fence from Uncle Sol's yard. One of the bulbs nearly hit their car! You'll never believe this—actually you probably will: they stopped the car and this kid started to run for the gate, but he didn't know exactly where it was so that slowed him down. It was Rocky and the police caught him red-handed, tearing up Uncle Sol's flowers.

"I should've known," David said pounding his open hand with his fist, "he always looked like a trouble-maker."

"Maaan, Uncle Sol said we should keep being nice to him, and look where it got Uncle Sol," Will added.

"Hey, there's more. The police put handcuffs on him and drove him right to the police station in the cruiser. I guess Rocky got to make one call, just like on TV, and he called his mom and get this, his grandfather said "Let 'im stay. Maybe it'll teach 'im a lesson.' He'll probably have to go to juvenile court, but Uncle Sol has to decide what he wants to do. I mean Uncle Sol could choose not to press charges—at least that's what my mother said."

"Oh, he should make that kid pay," Edie said, "I never liked him, right from the start."

"That's what *I* said, but Mom said it's up to Uncle Sol to decide." As the morning bus slowed to a stop and the kids started boarding, Jon added, "Oh—my mom also found out the reason they moved here. Rocky's dad died last year after being sick for a while. So they've moved in with his mom's parents. You'd think his life was bad enough without adding more, wouldn't ya?" The other kids just shook their heads in bewilderment as they took their seats.

Uncle Sol chose not to press charges against Rocky. The boy's mother insisted that he pay the full amount of replacing all the bulbs and any other damage that was done. Rocky did.

And she insisted that Rocky apologize to Uncle Sol, in person face-to-face, which he did. But from that moment on, Rocky made every effort to avoid going by Uncle Sol's house.

For a while, Rocky's mother drove him to school, but it wasn't long before Rocky was back on the bus with everyone else. The ring of empty seats around him as he rode the bus was larger than ever and not one of the neighborhood kids would even look at him. When the school bus passed the garden, Rocky couldn't help but notice how Uncle Sol was slowly putting the flowerbeds back together. Rocky knew he had ruined something wonderful, and even though he had paid the money for Uncle Sol to buy new flowers, he knew there was no way to recreate the garden and its pleasures this year.

He found himself really wanting to go into Uncle Sol's yard and feel welcomed like all the others. "I've ruined any chance I might have had for being welcomed there," Rocky thought as he stared out the school bus window. "The kids here hate me and I'm sure Uncle Sol does, too."

Uncle Sol watched for Rocky every day. He'd learned a lot more about Rocky and Rocky's family since the 'flower incident'. "The boy is just so lonesome for his dad and the life he used to have," the older neighbor said to Julie and Jon's mother one afternoon when she stopped her daily walk in front of his yard.

"But Uncle Sol, what he did was awful and there's no excuse for such out-of-control behavior. I don't want Jon thinking he can act like that just because he's mad."

"I know, I know what he did was very wrong. But he paid for the damage. I just hate to see him continue to suffer. He needs to feel included somewhere in his life," Uncle Sol responded.

Finally Uncle Sol saw an opportunity. Rocky was passing by his yard on the far side of the street, eyes looking straight at the ground in front of him, completely focused on the pavement about two feet in front of him. His concentration was so good that he was startled to find Uncle Sol standing right in front of him. He stopped, but continued staring at the ground.

Rocky didn't know what to say. "I'm sorry" just didn't seem to be enough. But before he could say anything, Uncle Sol said, "Look at me, Rocky." Slowly he lifted his head. Instead of the anger he expected, there was silence. Uncle Sol had a gentle smile on his face and just looked him right in the eyes. There was something kind and inviting in Uncle Sol's gaze and finally Rocky, stammered, "I'm really sorry for what I did. I don't even know why I did it … I…"

Before Rocky could finish, Uncle Sol just said, "I forgave you when you apologized before. Ah, listen are you heading somewhere right now? I mean, do you have somewhere you have to be?"

"No, I was just walkin' around.'

"Would you come on over to my yard? I'd like to move some lawn furniture and it's just too much to do by myself."

"Uh, sure. I can help you."

Uncle Sol led Rocky around to the backyard and together they moved the lawn glider underneath one of the large shade trees. "Ever been in one of these old-fashioned gliders, Rocky?" When the boy shook his head "no", Uncle Sol said, "Well, get in and try it. It beats trying to find strong enough tree branches for a two person swing." The teenager climbed into the glider that could easily seat four people and true to its name, it glided back and forth quietly and effortlessly. Rocky started to get up when he caught Uncle Sol just looking at him. The man just didn't quit caring, that was plain enough for Rocky to see and the teen just couldn't find the strength to fight off that kind of steady caring any more. He plopped back down on the seat of the glider.

"Uncle Sol, you got time to talk?"

"I do have time, Rocky. Mind if I sit down?" When the boy nodded his willingness to share the glider, Uncle Sol sat on the opposite side, away from Rocky, giving him as much room as possible.

"Uncle Sol, I wish I could tell you why I tore up your garden. I wish I understood it myself. I mean looking back, I can't think of a stupider thing I could have done. But at that moment ... well, I don't know..." Rocky's voice trailed off. He shook his head and then held his head in both hands as he rested his elbows on his knees. Staring at the moving grass beneath the glider, he just started talking, "For the longest time I've had this pressure in my chest that just never goes away. It's like I can't breathe easy anymore. And when I look at things, it's like all the color has gone out of the world. Everything is gray and it never gets better. I think, 'what's the point of making friends?' 'What's the point of talking to anybody?' I don't think I'll ever laugh or even smile again—not a real smile, not one that comes from the inside— 'cause it feels like the place where those smiles come from died the minute my dad died."

"Then on top of everything else, we moved in with Grandma and Grandpa. They mean well, but it's just really hard. This isn't home. I guess it has to be now, but it isn't my real home. It's nothing like my real home. Anyway, when I started passing by your house and I'd see you in the yard and I'd see all the kids and everyone seeming so happy all the time, like life's perfect or something—I don't know, it just made me mad. All I could think was 'it's not fair that he has this perfect life. It's not fair he's got the perfect yard with the perfect flowers'. It just kept coming into my mind how it's not fair that my dad died I had to leave my home and my neighborhood and my friends. Sometimes I just wanted to run over to the fence and yell at you, IT'S NOT FAIR! But I didn't 'cause I'd look like a lunatic or something..." He glanced sideways over at Uncle Sol with a crooked smile flickering on his lips before it disappeared. Uncle Sol just listened.

"But then a really awful day came." Rocky sat up again and looked at Uncle Sol. "At school, they have these forms that need to be filled out when you're moving from eighth grade to high school and they hand them out to make sure all the information's correct."

Uncle Sol was mostly just nodding his head to let Rocky know he was listening carefully, but he added, "I remember those from when my kids went through the school."

"Well, it was like getting a slap across the face right there in class. The paper had all the right information about my mother—her name, address, phone number, occupation, emergency numbers, all that stuff. And it had the right information about my dad, too," he added more quietly. "Across all those spaces for name, address, phone number, occupation, emergency numbers, there was this handwritten note in dark ugly black letters, 'DECEASED'. Man, I thought I was going to bust out crying in class. I mean, those people don't care … it's just a cold fact to them … but it's my dad they're talking about. I just wanted outta there. I came home and tried to make my head forget, but I didn't do so well at that. When I went to bed, I just couldn't sleep … again."

"So I got up and I put my clothes on and said to my mom, 'I'm goin' for a walk' and she said, 'uh huh'. Ya know, my mom was never like this before my dad died. She was interested in every thing I said and she always knew what I was doin', where I was goin' and who I was goin' with and she'd never have let me go out at night like that. Now it's like her body's around, but she's gone. Anyway, so I started walking and I walked by your house and it's like something in me snapped. I was thinkin' dumb thoughts like, 'There's The Perfect Neighbor's yard. Everything's just perfect in there. I bet his whole life is perfect. I bet he hasn't had a single bad thing ever happen to him. I bet his whole world has never been ripped apart.' That's when it happened. Not that it makes any sense now, but at the time, rippin' apart The Perfect Neighbor's perfect yard seemed like a perfectly logical thing to do." The flood of words finally trickled away and the only sound that could be heard was the rhythmic rolling of the glider on its tracks. "I know I've said it before, but really, I am very sorry about all the trouble I caused you."

"And as I've said before, your apology was accepted the very first time you offered it. Rocky, I've got another offer for you. I'd like you to feel absolutely free to come here any time."

"Even if you let me in, I don't think I'll feel very welcome with the rest of the kids around here. They hate me."

Rocky's back had been to the path that led around Uncle Sol's house into the backyard and he had entirely missed the small parade of kids who had walked around the corner, seen who was in the glider with Uncle Sol, and then disappeared. But Uncle Sol knew his young neighbors well. He knew they were probably within earshot, so he stood up and got off the glider and said to Rocky, "Rocky, everyone is welcome in this garden, no matter what. People make mistakes, sometimes big mistakes, but how can any of us show we've learned something if we aren't given a second chance? Trust me, there are no perfect kids around here. Plenty of *them* have had second chances with me ... even third chances and I'm sure you'll find a welcome around here sooner rather than later." Rocky got off the glider and Uncle Sol just extended his hand to shake Rocky's. As the teen returned the shake, Uncle Sol put his arm around Rocky's shoulder. "Rocky, I'll be very disappointed if you don't make it a habit to stop by here as often as you can. You know, after school, weekends ... I mean it."

After that, nearly every day after school Rocky could be found in Uncle Sol's yard helping Uncle Sol with his garden. Rocky talked a lot about his old home and his dad and he learned that Uncle Sol's wife had died of the same disease years earlier. He was finally able to say, "I guess your life isn't perfect after all."

"I never said it was, Rocky. I just have learned that I can trust my Maker with whatever happens." Rocky took it all in. He'd found his first real friend in the neighborhood.

It wasn't long before the neighborhood kids began to talk to Rocky and invite him to join their activities and even though he most often chose to hang out with Uncle Sol,

Rocky was beginning to smile more often. He was beginning to find his way with the help of a wise old neighbor.

Ephesians 2.8-10
Luke 15.4-7

Theological Foundation: see p.198
Guide for Non-religious Settings: see p.241

The Secret Artist

Everyone in the neighborhood loved the Christmas season, but Uncle Sol seemed to love it best. On Thanksgiving evening, he would light the electric candles in every window of his house. Before the first week of Advent was through, he hand-delivered Christmas cards to all the families in the neighborhood with small gifts of special cookies to "get the season off to a sweet start". Christmas wasn't just a "day" for Uncle Sol and really, it wasn't just a "season" either. For Uncle Sol, Christmas lasted the whole year. He was always doing kind little things for the neighbors, but especially for the neighborhood children. The children just loved him for the way he shared his home, his garden and his knowledge about life and how to really love others.

It was about 12 days before Christmas, when Uncle Sol heard a knock at his front door just about suppertime. "I wonder who that could be?" Uncle Sol thought as he turned on the porch light and unlocked the door. By the time he'd turned on the light and opened the storm door to greet the "door-knocker", not a soul was in sight. Instead, he saw an old plastic grocery store bag tied to the stair railing.

"Well, what's this?" he wondered out loud as he untied the bag and brought it in. It certainly didn't look like a Christmas present and it didn't really occur to him that it might be one until he opened it in the kitchen. Inside the bag was a large ball of tissue paper. "Obviously, whatever it is must be fragile to require so much protective padding," he mused.

It took some effort to get through the layers of taped tissue paper, but he was rewarded for his trouble. Under all those layers of tissue he discovered a beautiful ceramic lamb that had been carefully painted by some young artist. Uncle

Sol just smiled as he examined the little painted face, the bright black hooves and the long tail. "I wonder which one of the neighborhood lambs did this?" He chuckled at his own play on words. "Obviously, he or she doesn't want me to know."

The next night, just about suppertime, there was a knock at the door again. Thinking nothing of the previous evening's mystery visitor, Uncle Sol turned on the light and opened the door to greet the 'door- knocker.' There was no one standing on the front steps, but a bag was hanging from the railing just like the night before. He brought the bag inside and once again, he found something wrapped in a huge ball of tissue paper. This time, when he unwrapped it, he discovered a ceramic shepherd. That's when he realized that someone was giving him a nativity scene.

The next night, it was the same thing: a knock at the door, a bag on the railing, another piece of the nativity scene. Night after night the plastic shopping bags were tied to the stair railing. A donkey, a camel and a cow joined the growing collection of sheep, shepherds and wise men. One by one each new piece was placed near the earlier arrivals on an old wooden table that Uncle Sol brought down from the attic.

Uncle Sol enjoyed giving mystery gifts himself so he understood the game of remaining undiscovered. Still, he couldn't help wanting to know who was being so kind and so clever. After the fifth delivery, he even tried waiting behind the curtains of the window in his darkened living room in hopes of catching a glimpse of the mystery "door-knocker". He never succeeded. But each night when he stepped out onto his front steps to untie the bag from the railing he would call out into the dark night, "Thank you, whoever you are."

At last, it was Christmas Eve. Uncle Sol's grown-up children and his grandchildren had all arrived for Christmas celebrations. They were getting ready to sit down to dinner when one of his granddaughters noticed he seemed a bit distracted.

"Grandpa, you keep looking at the door. Are you expecting someone?"

"Well, yes and no," he answered. Uncle Sol then told his whole family about the mysterious "door knocker".

"Every evening about supper time for the last ten days or so, there's been a knock at the door and since there's still one piece missing, I'm just waiting for the knock."

The entire family joined in the waiting. One of the granddaughters tried to fool everyone by knocking under the table. That sent a stampede of young grandchildren to the front door. "I'll catch the person who's been surprising you," promised his oldest grandson as they all returned to the dining room. All through the meal family members listened for the knock, but it never came. Uncle Sol was not only a little surprised but a little disappointed that the last gift had not arrived. He was puzzled about the absence of the "door knocker" on this last night before Christmas, since the last and most important piece was still missing. He tried not to let his disappointment show, though he remained puzzled as he joined his family in cleaning up the dinner dishes. Everyone agreed that as beautiful as the whole nativity scene was, it really looked quite empty without Baby Jesus.

Uncle Sol, his two sons and their wives and his daughter and her husband, along with the grandchildren went to the Christmas Eve service at the church. "I'll bet the 'door knocker' will leave the gift while we're away at church, Grandpa," his oldest granddaughter reassured him as they drove home. But when they arrived, there was no plastic bag hanging from the railing on the front steps awaiting them.

Christmas morning, Uncle Sol's grandchildren raced … not to their stockings, but to the front door to see if the plastic bag with Baby Jesus had now appeared. "It's got to be here today! It's Christmas morning!" the children exclaimed as they unlocked the front door. But in the clear, cold morning air, nothing was hanging on the stair rail. "There's nothing here, Grandpa … no bag, no note, nothing."

"Maybe whoever it is ran out of time and didn't finish all the painting," one of the grandchildren offered.

"Maybe he tripped on the way over here yesterday and fell and broke it," another suggested.

Uncle Sol pushed away the touch of disappointment that came over him. "Christmas is a wonderful day and today is especially wonderful because I have my whole family here … whether or not the mystery "door-knocker's" final gift ever comes," he said as he joined the grandchildren at the door.

"I'm sure whoever it is will eventually let me know," he said. "Come on, kids, let's get to those stockings." The children squealed with delight as they raced to the living room. Very quickly, everyone turned his or her attention to the gifts under the Christmas tree and the missing plastic bag was forgotten in the excitement of new toys, games and clothing.

"Here you go, Grandpa, another little box with your name on it," his granddaughter said as she carried a gift over to him.

"Gosh, Grandpa, you always get the most presents," his grown son teased. Uncle Sol smiled as he looked at the crayon-colored gift tag with the ragged letters of a beginning printer. Every year many of the children in the neighborhood used Christmas time to thank him for all that he had done throughout the year. Usually his gifts were picture books drawn by little hands, or something made during a Cub Scout or Brownie project. The tag on this box simply said, "To Uncle Sol, with love, Jenny."

As Uncle Sol took the box, he smiled. Jenny and her family had lived in the neighborhood for a long while, but early last spring, her father's National Guard unit had been deployed overseas and he was still not expected home for several months. Before leaving town, Jenny's father had talked with Uncle Sol about his concerns for his family. During those long conversations, Uncle Sol offered to not only help Jenny's family with the house and yard maintenance, but to just watch out for all of them while Jenny's father was away. So the older neighbor checked in on them every couple of days. During the summer, he had taught Jenny's mother how to change spark plugs on lawn mowers and do all kinds of other yard care. He knew they were grateful because they had fed him dinner on more than one occasion and Jenny, along with her little brother were always drawing pictures for him.

Uncle Sol had a hunch as he untied the ribbon from around the box and opened it. There, inside, was a small ball of tissue paper and along with it, a note. He unwrapped the tissue paper, already anticipating what was in it. Baby Jesus just smiled up at him from his manger bed. Uncle Sol unfolded the note,

"'A light shines in the darkness and the darkness cannot overcome it.' Thank you Uncle Sol for helping us keep that light in our lives since Daddy's been gone. With love, Jenny and my whole family."

Uncle Sol blinked back a tear and then cleared his throat. "It looks like the honored guest has arrived," he said as he held up the last piece of the nativity scene for all to see. The entire family escorted Baby Jesus to the center of the table where he joined all the other pieces. Uncle Sol's grown-up children knew that even as they placed the ceramic Baby Jesus right in the middle of all the other figures, the real Christ Child was very much alive in their father's heart and was still bringing joy to the world one family at a time in the neighborhood.

Matthew 2:1-12
Luke 2:1-19

Theological Foundation: see p.200

Trusting the Clues

Nobody believed Will. He was always teasing people so when he said, "I'm the clue," all his neighborhood friends just laughed while they continued looking for the piece of brown paper with directions on it. The children were right in the middle of a treasure hunt that Edie had asked Uncle Sol to make up for her birthday party.

It all started some weeks back when the children were sitting on Uncle Sol's deck after school. The warm sunshine, the coming vacation from school, the peanut butter cookies and milk worked together to put everyone into a talkative mood.

"You know what I liked to do when I was little? I liked to sneak up on people. It was really funny when I'd be so quiet that my mom had no idea that I had gotten right behind her. When she turned around … oh, she would jump and then she'd yell, 'David, don't do that!'" David laughed as he told the others.

"Well, don't do that to me, David. I'd probably have a heart attack!" The twinkle in Uncle Sol's eyes assured David that his elderly neighbor was joining in the fun.

"I liked to climb up in the tree in our yard as high as I could go so that no one could see me and then I'd wait until everyone was looking for me before I'd sneak down and get back in the house. I'd sit down at the kitchen table and just wait for them to find me in the house. Oh, they'd get so mad trying to figure out where my hiding place was. It was great!" Will smiled such a self-satisfied smile that Julie gave him a playful shove with her foot as Uncle Sol said, "I always had a hunch when your family was looking for you, you'd joined the birds again, Will."

That's when Edie spoke up, "What *I* liked to do was make up treasure hunts for Paul and Helen. I'd take a toy and some crackers, hide them in a little wooden box I had. Then I'd make up clues about how to find it." Edie laughed, "I always had to read the clues to them because they were still so little they couldn't read for themselves. They'd run all over the house looking in all the places I'd hidden the treasure box before."

That's when everyone's eyes lit up. "Hey, that's a great idea ... Let's have a big treasure hunt." "Yeah, we could use the whole neighborhood." "We should have real treasure, too! You know, gold, jewels." Laughter filled the air as the friends shared their extravagant suggestions.

"I used to make up big treasure hunts for my kids and their friends when they were younger. It got to be a birthday tradition for us and every year the clues got harder just so it'd still be a challenge," said Uncle Sol .

"How about making up one for my birthday, Uncle Sol? I'd love it." Edie asked

"Well, I think I could do that, Edie." There was a long pause as Uncle Sol let that settle around the circle. "Actually, I'd like to do that. I've already got some ideas."

"You've got to invite me!" Will yelled.

"Me, too" echoed David. All the other children on Uncle Sol's deck pleaded to be invited.

"Can we invite the whole neighborhood, Uncle Sol?" Edie's quizzical look mirrored her question.

"Well, of course we can. Why would we leave anyone out of the best treasure hunt this neighborhood has seen in years?" the elder neighbor asked.

Uncle Sol went right to work on the treasure hunt. As afternoon flowed into evening, he thought long and hard after walking all around the neighborhood. "Let's see, Edie's friends are so close to being teens, this hunt ought to take some time. Hmmmm ... brown paper, brown markers..."

The next afternoon Edie stopped by Uncle Sol's house. Before she could ring the doorbell, she heard her elder neighbor chuckling. When he answered the door, Edie asked, "What were you laughing at, Uncle Sol?"

"Oh, I was chuckling at one of my clues. It *is* a good one if I do say so myself."

"What is it?" Edie asked, hoping that she might just catch Uncle Sol off guard.

"Oh, no you don't. No insider information for this treasure hunt even if it is for your birthday," he laughed. "Now what brings you here today?"

"My mother said she doesn't want you doing every part of the birthday party preparations all by yourself and wants you to give her a call. I actually think she wants to get in on the secrets of making up treasure hunts. You know, Uncle Sol, I think this is going to be the best birthday party I've had!" With that Edie bounded off the steps down the front walk. "See ya, Uncle Sol." With a wave she was gone.

Two weeks later, the big day arrived. It seemed like the whole neighborhood had been counting the days until Edie's birthday.

This was no easy hunt. Uncle Sol's choice of brown paper made it especially difficult to actually see the hidden clues. And *that* only became a challenge after they had figured out the meaning of the rhyme which gave them a hint as to the location of the next clue. Just for an example, one clue was this: "Lapping sounds put me to sleep and wake me up. If I sleep one way I'm a shelter; if I sleep another, I'm a cup." That was the clue for the canoe that was tied to the tree in Alice's yard beside the lake. And *that* was one of the *easy* ones!

Uncle Sol had told the children that the treasure hunt would take awhile, but no one, least of all Edie was expecting it to take the two hours they had already spent. They were only just now at the last clue ... or at least they thought they were at the last clue. But there was no paper ... nothing. They had solved the riddle that said, "No hammer on anvil sings a song, those old days are all long gone, but branches still spread to form shade dark as night, the clue you all seek will lead you just right." Jon's memory of a poem that his parents had read to him when he was little about a village blacksmith and a spreading chestnut tree led the whole pack of treasure seekers to the chestnut tree in Uncle Sol's yard. They had searched all around the tree and under the rocks that were near the trunk and they had even gotten on their hands and knees crawling around looking for the brown piece of paper with the answer.

"When we find this clue, it will lead us to the treasure, because Uncle Sol said there were twelve clues to the treasure and we are at #12."

"This one will do it, for sure. We're *so* close!"

"Come on everyone, keep looking!"

Finally, David said, "Will, you're not doing anything to help us look. Do you already know where the clue is?"

All Will said in response was, "I'm the clue."

"You're not the clue; clues look like this," said David waving a handful of brown paper strips in Will's face. Will didn't say anything more and the treasure seekers kept looking and then they finally decided that Jon had been wrong and that it couldn't be the chestnut tree. They ran off to search under another big tree near the lake.

Will had been with the treasure seekers all along, but when they left the shade of the chestnut tree he stayed right there. It wasn't long before Edie came back, alone.

"Will, aren't you going with us to look for the clue?"

"I'm the clue," Will said again.

"You said that before. How can you be the clue?"

"I'm the clue," was all Will said in response.

Edie just stared at Will for a long time and then she slowly said, "Well, if you're the clue, how do I get to the treasure?"

Will smiled and said, "Follow me."

Will led Edie down the sliding hill that the neighborhood children used all winter, then he looked very carefully at all the bushes and trees at the bottom of the hill.

All of a sudden he slipped under some bushes and called to Edie. She, too, slipped under the bushes and followed Will's voice. The undergrowth was thick, but there almost seemed to be a path, maybe made by rabbits or even deer; but whatever it was, it was certainly narrow and almost impossible to see. Just when Edie thought her back would never straighten out because she had to be so bent over to follow Will, the bushes disappeared. Right in front of her was the whole lake. It was a part of the lake she'd never seen. There were no houses in sight and the only sound that Edie could hear was her favorite music coming from the middle of a giant tree. She walked over to the tree and looked up. Through the leafy branches she could see the floor of what looked like a tree house…

"Hey, Will, what's this?" Edie asked eagerly. She turned around and Will was no where to be found. He had disappeared into the bushes.

"Will?!" "Will!?" Fear began to creep its way into her mind, but just then a familiar voice spoke out.

"Edie? Edie, is that you?"

"Yes, yes, Uncle Sol … but where are you?" Edie's eyes were searching the shore, the bushes…

"Up here … I'm up in the tree house … come on up." Uncle Sol leaned out the window of the tree house smiling and motioning her to climb up. Edie's momentary fear evaporated. Once up in the tree house, Edie was ecstatic. "Uncle Sol, I can't believe this! Wow, this is an amazing treasure … a tree house, a cake…" The tree house had a table and chairs in it and on the table was a cake. Next to the cake was a box that looked just like a treasure.

"Open the treasure box," Uncle Sol said.

"Ohhhhh" was all that Edie could say as she followed his instructions. The box was filled with bracelets, necklaces, armbands and pendants made with intricate beads and twine.

"Choose whichever one you would like and then just wait with me. The others will be here soon."

Sure enough, the loud laughter of the rest of the treasure seekers could be heard in the bushes and underbrush. Suddenly Will burst through into the clearing around the tree house. "Uncle Sol, they finally figured it out; they finally believed me," he said with a grin, having enjoyed being Uncle Sol's secret accomplice.

"Okay, now one at a time. This tree house can't hold all of you at once!" One by one, the party-goers scrambled into the tree house and collected their treasure with Edie helping them make their choices. "That's beautiful on you, Jenny. You need to take that one." "Oh, Jon, I think that armband makes you look like a pirate. That has to be yours!" Uncle Sol got two of the boys to help him take the cake down from the tree house. Edie's mother appeared with all the supplies for a great birthday celebration—juice and balloons, birthday plates and cups. A loud and off-key rendition of "Happy Birthday" echoed across the lake.

"How did you ever find this place, Uncle Sol?" Jon finally asked when nearly everyone had finished eating. "I mean, I thought I knew where everything was around the neighborhood, but I've never seen this."

"I was helping Nick look for Kristy when she disappeared one day. I followed her barking and that's when I stumbled on the deer trail and followed it here. I was really surprised myself. And this is where I found Kristy. She had tree-housed a raccoon." I could see that the tree house was really rugged. So when I got home I called Mr. Koth and found out that he'd built it for his grandchildren a few years ago and he still takes care of it. I asked if I could use it for this little surprise and he was happy to have us end the treasure hunt here."

"I'd never have found it, Uncle Sol, if I hadn't asked Will about being a clue. That was pretty sneaky—using a person," Edie playfully scolded.

"Well, it was either use a person or pave the entire path with brown paper," Uncle Sol responded with a shrug of his shoulders and the ever-present twinkle in his eye.

"Hey, Uncle Sol, it was so much easier following Will … once we figured out the real clue at that tree," David added. Everyone nodded.

"I know what we could do next, Uncle Sol." Excitement was building in Jenny's voice. "We could do a whole new kind of treasure hunt where the only clues are people." David was quick to join in, "Yeah and each one could tell you only one thing about the location of the treasure." Then it was Will's turn, "Oh! Oh! And we could start with a list of possible people, who might have the clues, but some would and some wouldn't…"

Uncle Sol knew where this was going as he finished his last bite of cake. He just leaned back against the tree trunk and let his young neighbors' imaginations soar.

John 14:1-14

Theological Foundation: see p.202
Guide for Non-religious Settings: see p.243

Seeing the Truth

"Uncle Sol! Uncle Sol!" Frantic voices filled the neighborhood street. The children's voices were mixed with the unmistakable sound of a dog yelping in terrible pain. Uncle Sol had been reading the newspaper on his deck when he'd heard a screech of tires. He'd already started to get up when he heard his name being called, mixed with the agonizing cries of a wounded animal. Will and Jon came racing around the side of the house.

"Uncle Sol, you've gotta come quick," they blurted out, gasping for air. "It's Kristy, she's been hit." Kristy was one of the neighborhood dogs. She lived with Nick's family, but she belonged to everyone. She played with any and all of the children whenever they were outside. She watched from the window when they left for school and she was waiting in the exact same spot when the children got off the school bus. When Nick dropped off his school bag, he always let Kristy out to play. That usually wasn't a problem, but today Kristy had seen a squirrel dash across the street just as Nick let her out the door and she had leaped off the front steps and run across the street after the squirrel, right in front of Mrs. Vardis' car.

By the time Uncle Sol got to the street, Myra Vardis was out of her car kneeling beside the dog and trying to comfort Nick. When she saw Uncle Sol she jumped to her feet, "Uncle Sol, I didn't have time to stop. I was just driving down the street toward home and then out of nowhere, there was Kristy, right in front of me. I don't know what else I could have done. I feel horrible, just horrible. I've never hit anything before." Myra fumbled in her pocket and used the tissue she found to wipe her eyes.

"Accidents happen, Myra. It's not your fault." said Uncle Sol as his eyes were scanning the scene. Myra's focus darted from the dog on the road, to Nick, to her year old twins, Jill and Ross, who were starting to cry in their car seats. Children were streaming from all parts of the neighborhood forming a circle around the car and injured dog. Nick was on his knees rocking back and forth over his crumpled pet.

"What'd ya think, Uncle Sol? Is Kristy gonna die?" Nick's eyes were swimming with tears he wouldn't let escape here in front of all these people. Uncle Sol bent down to look at the wheezing animal. Kristy tried to get up, but her hind legs wouldn't support her and she collapsed with a yelp and began to pant wildly.

"It's okay, girl, easy, easy. Just settle down." Uncle Sol's voice soothed the injured dog as he carefully stroked her face and neck. Just the sound of his voice began to soothe the anxious children, too. Except for the Vardis twins.

"Myra, there's no reason for you to stay. The twins aren't going to stand for much more waiting in car seats, you know," Uncle Sol said turning to the young mother whose day had been turned upside down.

"You'll call me, Uncle Sol, if there's anything I can do?" she asked as she got into her car.

Uncle Sol nodded and motioned the children to move out of the way so Mrs. Vardis could pass. With the car out of the way, the children closed in around Nick, Uncle Sol and Kristy. The only sound that could be heard was the frantic panting and the scraping of the dog's feet as she tried once again to get up.

"Hold on there, Kristy," said Uncle Sol as he stroked her head and worked his hands down her chest. After checking her front legs and getting no reaction, he began to slowly stroke her sides and back. Right at the point where her hind legs joined the back, she yelped and then tried to bite at Uncle Sol's hand. "She's hurt her hip on this side, Nick. See how she let's me know not to touch that any more?" With a little more gentle probing, Uncle Sol was fairly certain that not only was Kristy's hip damaged, but the leg was probably broken, as well. Her breathing was getting shallower and her eyes were glazing over, but she struggled to focus on Uncle Sol as he spoke softly to her.

"Nick, is your mother at home?" Uncle Sol asked.

"No, she won't be home until suppertime, but my older brother will be here soon."

"Well, I think we've got to get Kristy to a vet right away. I can drive you."

Nick looked relieved and scared and grateful all at the same time. Uncle Sol hurried back to his house and returned with his van. He stopped beside the huddle of children and then handed Nick a blanket as he stepped out of the driver's seat.

"Nick, I'm going to lift Kristy and when I have her off the ground enough, I want you to slide the blanket under her, okay?"

"Okay."

"Now she's going to yelp because it'll hurt her, but don't let that stop you. If she bites at me, don't worry I'll be fine." In one swift move, Uncle Sol lifted the injured dog enough for Nick to get the blanket underneath her and then he set her down again. "Good, now let's each pick up one end of the blanket and we'll transport her to the van that way."

The young owner and the old neighbor each took one end of the blanket and lifted the dog into the back of Uncle Sol's van.

Once they had reached the veterinary hospital, Kristy was taken right into an examining room. "She's going into shock," the vet said, as she gave the animal a shot. Nick cringed as he watched the needle puncture his dog's leg, but she hardly moved. The vet examined Kristy carefully and concluded that there were broken bones in the leg and the hip. "I think she's got some internal bleeding, too, but I can't be sure how extensive that is. It all depends on whether the broken bones punctured anything. I'll need some x-rays and some other tests to see how much damage there really is." Nick called his mother and she authorized the vet to do whatever was necessary to save the family pet.

"Nick, there really isn't anything more you can do right now. I've got assistants who'll help me with Kristy. I'll call you at home when I know more." The vet was sympathetic to the young teen's misery, but she wanted to turn her full attention to the injured animal. "Give Kristy a good luck pat," the vet urged as she quickly moved Kristy to another room.

"Let's go home, Nick," Uncle Sol finally said. The ride back to the neighborhood was quiet. Nick was staring out the window, clearly thinking hard about his dog. At last the silence was broken,

"Uncle Sol, Kristy was looking so much weaker when we left, like she was fading away. I'm afraid she's going to die." Nick quickly looked away and wiped something off his cheek as he got out of the car at his house.

"I noticed that too, Nick. But I think she'll pull through."

Around suppertime there was a knock at Uncle Sol's door. When he opened it, he found Nick standing there, shoulders sagging, eyes glistening with tears on the edge of spilling over. "Come in, Nick. What's the news?"

"Oh, Uncle Sol…" he couldn't go on. Nick bit his lower lip trying to hold back the crying that wanted to come out. Uncle Sol reached out and put his hand on Nick's shoulder. The boy buried his face in Uncle Sol's extended arm. "The vet called. .Kristy's really bad … she's not going to make it … through the night." The words came out in short bursts between the muffled sobs of the broken-hearted young teenager. Uncle Sol just waited for the wave of sorrow to pass. Nick looked up and wiped his eyes with the backs of his hands. "Uncle Sol, why?"

"Why what, Nick? Why accidents? Why injuries? Why sickness? Why death? There are no answers for those kinds of questions, Nick. At least not answers that make sense to our hearts. Why don't you tell me what the vet said again."

"She said there was a lot more internal damage than she first thought and that Kristy is really struggling. She suggested to my mom and dad they put Kristy to sleep, but they wanted to wait until tomorrow. That's when the vet said Kristy probably wouldn't live through the night. I just hate for my dog to be all alone at the vet's while she's dying."

"Now, Nick don't go burying your dog before she's dead."

"What'd ya mean, Uncle Sol?"

"Just that, don't bury your dog before she's dead. She's not dead yet."

"No, but nobody's holding much hope that she'll be here in the morning."

"I am, Nick. I am holding out hope that she'll be here in the morning. We'll just have to wait and see."

Nick trudged home and began his vigil. He lay awake and watched the clock pass from ten o'clock to eleven to midnight. He fell asleep and waked up over and over again. Each time he would pull the clock close to his face so that he could read the time. It was the longest night of his life. With each passing hour he realized that it was an hour closer to daylight. When he finally got out of bed, he felt weak and frightened. He was certain he would never be able to concentrate at school and secretly hoped his mother would let him stay home. He heard the phone ring through his bedroom door. The house grew silent as Nick, his brother and his father came into the kitchen to listen in on the conversation.

"...really? okay ... well, that's encouraging ... thank you so much for calling so early." Nick's mother hung up the phone and turned to her waiting family.

"Kristy made it through the night and she's lifting her head and looking around. She even drank a little water. The vet says Kristy's got quite a ways to go, but surviving last night was the most critical thing. She's encouraged."

Nick gulped down his cereal and juice and raced up to his room to get his backpack. "What's the rush, Nick? You've got plenty of time before the bus."

"I've got to tell Uncle Sol about Kristy before I go to school," he answered his mother as he dashed out the door. Nick ran all the way to Uncle Sol's house with the heavy backpack bouncing wildly on his shoulders. "Hey, Uncle Sol, Uncle Sol! Kristy made it through the night!" the boy announced as his older neighbor opened the door.

"That's great news, Nick. Anything else? Well, the vet said Kristy tried to drink some water and that she was looking around. That's Kristy all right, always curious about what's goin' on. The vet said that it would still be awhile before she was 'outta the woods', but the worst was last night and she made it."

Uncle Sol patted Nick on the shoulder. "That is really good news ... a great way to start the morning, I'd say."

"Yeah it is, but now I'm exhausted. I hardly slept last night I was so worried. Which brings me to something I was thinking a lot about in the night. Uncle Sol, you seemed really hopeful that Kristy would survive last night even when the vet and none of us in my family thought she would. How come?"

"Ohhh, it comes from years of watching, Nick. It's something I've come to see in the eyes of people, but I can see it in the eyes of some animals, too. How shall I describe it? When I look into people's eyes, I often can get a very good picture of their heart. It's like I can see what they're made of. I can tell if they are full of hope and trust or if they are fearful and discouraged. I can see whether or not they love life enough to fight for it. Now that's no guarantee they'll overcome an injury or an illness that threatens their life, but when I see that, I've learned to expect the unexpected. I saw that in Kristy's eyes yesterday right after she was hit. I knew she would make every effort to live and come back to her family."

"Well, Uncle Sol, you saw what the rest of us missed."

"I try not to look at just what's in front of me, Nick. I always try to look into the heart. That's where I find the truth of what's going on."

"Can you teach me to look that way, too, Uncle Sol?"

"Eventually, Nick. It takes time. Uh, something you don't have much of right now, neighbor. There's the bus!" Nick bolted down the street to the bus stop, while the children boarding the bus cheered him on.

1 Samuel 16.7; Psalm 139; Matthew 15:10-20
Theological Foundation: see p.204
Guide for Non-religious Settings: see p.245

The Boy Who Would Be King

"I can touch the clouds with my feet," David yelled as he pulled back hard on the chains of the swing, forcing his feet high into the air as he climbed to the top of the arc. Taking careful aim with his shoes, he tapped at the sky with his feet as if he were really tiptoeing on the tops of clouds before swinging back to earth.

"Hey, watch me, David! I can go even higher than you!" Jon leaned back as far as he could while still holding onto the chains. His feet did go even higher than David's as the chain suddenly went slack for a moment while Jon swung past the top of the bar that securely held the swings. The two friends were always trying to push the limits of the swing set in David's back yard.

"How far can you jump?" David challenged as he launched himself off the moving swing. The boy landed on his feet, but then tumbled to the ground from the force of his momentum. He scrambled back to the place where his feet first touched. "See if you can jump past here," he called out to his friend.

Jon kept swinging, gaining height with every pump of his legs. "All right, here I gooooooo," Jon flew through the air and barely touched his feet to the ground before rolling across the lawn.

"Ha! I still beat you, Jon! Just look where the grass's dented from your feet!" Jon's marks were a couple of inches short of David's. "I win, I win!" David crowed. "Let's do it again!" The boys raced each other back to the swings.

"When I grow up I'm gonna be the King," David announced as he swung past Jon. "Whatever I say, people will have to do it, because I'm the King."

"Well, when I grow up I'm gonna be rich!" Jon countered. "I'm gonna be so rich that you'll have to ask me for money even if you *are* the king!"

"Kings always have the most riches and they tell everybody what to do," David insisted as they passed each other, "so you'll have to listen to me!"

"Y' got that wrong, David. Kings have to listen to the people with the money and I'm going to be richer than you so you'll have to do what *I* say," Jon shot back.

"No, I won't!" David was getting madder by the moment.

"Yes, you will!" Jon repeated.

"No, I won't!"

"Yes, you will!"

The boys were yelling so much that Uncle Sol looked over the fence from his yard to see what was going on. Uncle Sol was everyone's adopted uncle. The children loved him and the children's parents loved him, too. Actually, it was impossible to find anyone who didn't love Uncle Sol. His gentle, wise ways with all of the people in the neighborhood won him the respect of young and old alike. He never liked to hear friends fighting and he could tell this argument was not going to accomplish anything.

"Hey boys, what's goin' on that two good friends like you are yelling so loudly?" The boys jumped off the swings and raced each other to the fence, each wanting to be the first one to tell his side of the argument to Uncle Sol.

"Uncle Sol, David said he's gonna be the most important man because he's gonna be King when he grows up and people will have to listen to whatever he says," Jon complained.

"Yeah, but Jon says he's gonna be the *richest* man in the world when *he* grows up and that rich men are more important than kings because kings need the rich men's money!" David hurled back.

Uncle Sol chuckled and leaned against the fence. "So that's what this is about? Who's gonna be the greatest when he's grown up?"

"Yeah, that's right. I say it's a king and Jon says it's a rich man," David said, summing up the conflict.

"So, who's right, Uncle Sol? Am I right or is David right?" Jon pressed.

"Jon, David, let me tell you a little secret." The older neighbor leaned across the fence and said in a loud whisper, "Kings and rich men will never be the greatest leaders." The furrowed foreheads and wrinkled noses on both boys' faces left no doubt that they found Uncle Sol's words very hard to believe.

Uncle Sol could easily see that getting this idea planted into the minds of two aspiring rulers of the world would not be easy.

"Why don't you boys come around to the deck in my yard and I'll tell you why I know I'm right and both of you are wrong," he said with a laugh.

The two friends looked at each other, shrugged their shoulders and then bolted for the gate that gave David and his friends quick entry into Uncle Sol's yard.

"Okay, Uncle Sol," David said as the two boys bounded up the steps to the deck and flopped in the chairs, "how can you say that?"

"Here's what I'm saying, but I wasn't the first to say it: 'If you want to be the greatest, you must be willing to be the least important person of all. You must be willing to be just like a servant or a slave to others.'"

"Oh, come on, Uncle Sol. That was in Bible days, but that's not true today." Jon still wasn't willing to give in on his claim about rich men.

"Oh, quite the contrary," Uncle Sol said, remaining firm. "I can even tell you about someone who proved it was true just a few years ago."

"I'd like to hear that, because I still don't believe it," Jon said.

"This is a story about a girl named Agnes who was born in Albania."

"Ohhhh, now *there's* a name ... Agnes from Albania..." David teased

"Now, David ... Agnes is a very ancient Christian name and her parents wanted their little girl to have a strong name—just like your parents did when they named *you 'David'*.

"Okay, Uncle Sol, I'm sorry. I shouldn't make fun of names ... I know, I know." When David's face showed he really did understand, Uncle Sol nodded and then continued.

"Agnes decided to follow Jesus' idea. She decided to serve people just as Jesus had asked his disciples to do. When she was 18 years old she left her parents' home and joined a group of Catholic nuns. She got a little training to be a teacher before she was sent to India."

Uncle Sol interrupted his story to ask, "Do you boys know what Catholic nuns are?"

"No, not really," Jon answered.

"The Roman Catholic Church is one part of the Christian Church in the world. Some people who grow up in the Catholic Church choose to never marry and instead serve God with their whole lives. They make special promises to Jesus Christ and to the Church and the women who do this are called nuns. And that's what Agnes did."

"I have a friend who goes to the Catholic Church and she talks about this nun who teaches some of her religion classes. I think my friend really likes her."

"That's the idea. Agnes chose to be a nun and, as I said, she was sent to India. When she arrived in the city of Calcutta she began teaching high school. Every day for 17 years she walked to the school. She saw how the very poor were not able to get help from anybody, anywhere. She later said she knew in her heart that Jesus wanted her to help the poor. So that's what she did: she became a servant to the poorest of the poor who lived on the streets of that huge city. She moved out of her nice house that all the nuns shared and moved into the slums near where they lived.

"All this time, she still kept teaching at the school. It wasn't long before she had so much work to do that she didn't have time to teach there any longer. Finally, she was allowed to start her own group of nuns whose only work was to help the poor. Her group—it's actually called an 'order' in the Catholic Church—was named, 'Missionaries of Charity'. She started outdoor schools for the children who lived on the streets. Her friends worked with her to open centers to help the blind and elderly and people who had leprosy."

"I thought that was a skin disease that people got back in Bible days. I didn't know people could still get it!" David broke in.

"Didn't leprosy make people lose fingers and toes? Isn't that why people were so afraid of them?" Jon asked.

"It is a terrible skin disease, but modern medicine has done a lot to prevent the awful things that used to happen to people who caught it. Many people can be cured and that's what Agnes wanted to make available to the people who had the disease in Calcutta."

"Now, back to my point: The more she helped the poor, the more others began to notice what she was doing. The government of India gave her a special award for all her services to the people of India. She was given a ceremonial limousine and she raffled it off and used the money from it to help her pay for the home she was building for people with leprosy."

"Are you serious? She was given a limo and she just gave it away? Was it one of the 'stretch limos' that take famous people to big events? " Jon was amazed.

"Well, I'm not sure if it was a 'stretch limo', but she didn't exactly give it away. People bought tickets for a chance to win it, and then when the winner was chosen from all the tickets Agnes kept the money from the ticket sales and the winner took the limo."

"Whoa," Jon was still having a hard time imagining just walking away from a huge, fancy car.

"Her own church, The Roman Catholic Church, honored her for all her work. Then in 1979, the whole world honored her work and service to the poor by giving her the Nobel Peace Prize for humanitarian work."

"I know all this happened before you boys were even born, but she actually was alive during your very early years. She tried to resign as the leader of her order when she got quite old and sick, but people wouldn't hear of it. There was a vote and there was only one person who voted 'no', she should not be the head of the order any more. Do you know whose vote it was?"

"How could we know that, Uncle Sol?" Jon asked.

"I just thought you might try to guess who would've voted 'no'...."

"Well, the way you're asking, Uncle Sol, it must have been Agnes herself," David said.

"You're right."

"So she was the only one who didn't want her to keep being the leader?" Jon shook his head and smiled.

"That's right. Finally she just got too sick to keep leading the order and she retired, but she stayed right there with all the people she had loved and served all her life. She died in 1997; not that long ago, really."

"When Agnes died, her order had grown so large that there were 4000 nuns and hundreds of thousands of lay workers—that's volunteers—serving God in more than 90 countries."

"Oh, and just one more thing, she stopped using the name Agnes. When she became a Catholic nun she was given a new name, Sister Mary Teresa. The world came to know her as Mother Teresa."

"Mother Teresa? Really? My mom has a framed quote of hers hanging in the kitchen. It says something like 'maybe you can't do great things, but you can do small things with great love.' My mom really likes that. She says it all the time. So ... Agnes is Mother Teresa?"

"Yes, she is." Uncle Sol responded. "Now fellas, one hundred years from now not many people are gonna remember the names of this year's presidents or kings or the ten richest men in the world. I'll guarantee you, though, that people from all over the world will remember Mother Teresa for a very, very long time. She was a true leader—all because she followed what Jesus said about leadership. So if you want to be the greatest of all, you must be the servant of all."

All of a sudden David's eyes began to sparkle the way they always did when he had an idea. The boy jumped to his feet. "Uncle Sol, would you like some help with your garden?"

Jon jumped up beside him, "I could help you even better than David. I'm taller and stronger!"

"No, you're not stronger! You may be taller, but you're not stronger!" David scowled at Jon.

"Yes, I am," Jon insisted.

"Boys, boys! There's plenty of work for both of you in the garden. You can help me any time you want." As the boys raced to the garage for tools, Uncle Sol followed, shaking his head. "This lesson is gonna take a long time to teach…"

Mark 10:35-45

Theological Foundation: see p.206

THE SLIDING HILL

Uncle Sol had the best sliding hill in the whole neighborhood. His huge backyard seemed to be "made for children". At the back of the yard, past the grassy area that was good for soccer or Wiffle® ball or touch football, there was a steep slope. Standing at the edge of the slope, it was easy to see how fast sleds could get going before they reached the bottom where the flat area gave children plenty of time to stop before they got to the hedge at the very back of Uncle Sol's land. Winter after winter the children in the neighborhood would head for Uncle Sol's yard bringing their sleds, their snowboards and anything else that would slide down a hill. The older children would use the hill to practice jumping with their snowboards, while the younger ones just enjoyed the straight ride down the hill on their sleds, saucers, inner tubes and skis.

As the children got older, they were always tempted to try more and more daring maneuvers, often putting the younger ones at risk. Over the years, Uncle Sol had appointed a number of the older children to be "protectors" at the beginning of each winter's sliding season. Everyone knew it was a special privilege to be asked. It was no surprise after the first snowfall of the season when Uncle Sol asked Edie to be this year's "protector". Edie was one of the older children in the neighborhood. She was a natural leader and quite capable of watching out for the safety of others.

"Now Edie, you understand what I expect of a 'protector'?" Uncle Sol had asked.

"Yes, I think so. I'm supposed to make sure that the little kids get a chance to slide down the hill without any of the older ones taking away their turn, or cutting them off once they start sliding or scaring them by coming too close."

"And what do you do if you ask kids to take turns and the older ones or even the younger ones ignore you?"

"I'm supposed to come to you," Edie responded quickly, "like Rocky and my brother did when they were 'protectors'."

"That's right and the reason I want you to do that is because I will take responsibility for enforcing the rules for using my sliding hill. I don't want you to have to do that. Is that clear?"

"Yeah. I'm glad. That makes it pretty easy for me, Uncle Sol. I'll just watch the younger kids and make sure they're safe."

"Thank you, Edie. I just want everyone to enjoy the hill as much as my own children did when they were young," Uncle Sol concluded.

So after the first few snowfalls, Edie the "protector", watched over Helen, Julie, Jenny and all the others when they came to play in the snow. She made sure that the youngest ones were safe when they went sliding off down the hill. She made sure that the older ones gave way and avoided endangering the younger ones. But eventually, Edie the "protector" just got tired of paying attention to the younger children. She got tired of making sure everyone went down the hill in the order they were standing in line. She got tired of sorting out who was next and making sure the older ones were controlled in their acrobatics down the slope. She got really tired of having so few turns down the hill herself. And after a particularly fine snowfall, she finally made up her mind that it was time for the older kids to just take over the hill for the afternoon.

"Julie, you and your friends can't slide today," Edie announced as the small group of younger children bounded through Uncle Sol's backyard gate after school.

"Why not? It snowed last night," Julie responded. Edie thought fast, scrambling for a believable response: "Well, it was windy and uh, uh, there are lots of icy spots and you're not big enough to control your sled with the ice. You just shouldn't take the chance today, especially because Uncle Sol is away for the afternoon and it would take longer to get help if you got hurt. I'm sure we'll have more snow soon and the hill will be just right."

Julie and her friends were sure that Edie was being too protective, but what could they do? She was the "protector" Uncle Sol had chosen so they turned around and slowly walked out the gate. Compared to the excitement of sliding down the hill, there wasn't much else worth doing on a winter's afternoon. The disappointed band of the neighborhood's littler children wandered out along the sidewalk in front of Uncle Sol's house, hoping one of them could think of something else they could do.

Edie turned away and smiled. "That was easier than I thought it would be. Now we can really enjoy the hill without having to worry about hitting the little kids or stand around so long waiting for our turns." Edie, David, Will, Jon, Alice and the other older kids flew down the hill on their boards and tubes over and over again without the annoyance of having to wait for anybody.

Then the boys began making a huge jump, wrecking the smooth surface of the slope by digging and dragging more and more snow for their supreme challenge. From Edie's point of view, it seemed that the boys were really messing things up. They were making holes all over the place just for their jump and being really loud and getting in the way of Edie and her girlfriends.

"Hey, David, Uncle Sol doesn't want you guys digging up all his snow and making that huge jump. It won't be safe for the little kids when they come back so you'd better just break up that big jump now and make it safe again."

"Did Uncle Sol tell us to do that?" David demanded.

"Well, yes. Yes he did. I mean Uncle Sol made me this year's 'protector' and he told me to keep the little ones safe. That is definitely not safe for any of the little kids who slide here and you've dug so many holes, there's no good place to go around it!" Edie was firm and convincing.

David just looked at Edie with narrowed eyes. Edie didn't back down as she glared right back. There was something about Edie when she was mad that just made everyone else back away slowly as if they were backing away from a growling dog.

David held her stare a moment longer and then turned away, calling his friends over to help take down the huge jump. After filling in some of the holes, the boys just left; all the fun was gone. Now there was plenty of room for Edie and her friends. They played on the hill all afternoon with no interference from anyone.

When Uncle Sol got home, he thought it was rather odd that all the little neighborhood children were standing around just outside his yard half-heartedly building a snowman. Then he noticed the older boys throwing snowballs at the tree trunks and each other. After parking his van in the garage, he came around the front sidewalk and asked the clump of children hovering near his garden gate,

"Hey, what are all of you doing here? The snow is wonderful; the sun is out, why aren't you on the hill?" Uncle Sol asked.

"Because Edie said it was too icy for us. She said it was dangerous and that we might not be able to control our sleds very well," replied Julie. Then David chimed in,

"Yeah, and she said we just messed things up too much."

"Who did you say said that?" asked Uncle Sol.

"Edie did," they all said in unison.

"Oh, I see," said Uncle Sol. "You wait here. I'll be back for you very soon." With that Uncle Sol stepped through the garden gate and headed down the path to the hill at the back of his yard. Uncle Sol could see Edie and her friends having a wonderful time. In fact, Edie the "protector" was having such a wonderful time that she had entirely forgotten that she had told the others they couldn't play.

"Hi, Uncle Sol! This is the best the hill's ever been!" Edie called out in a loud voice from the bottom of the hill. He watched his "protector" climb the hill and then motioned to her to come over to the picnic table he left out all winter so the children would have a place to put their gear.

"I'm glad you're having such a great time today, Edie, but I do have an important question I need answered."

"Sure, Uncle Sol. What's the question?"

"If the hill is the best it's ever been, why are there so many children just outside my front yard with very sad faces?"

A little of Edie high spirits began to fade. "Well, I thought the hill wasn't quite right for the youngest ones today," she answered with an authority she was not now feeling. "And the boys were wrecking the whole hill because they were digging up the snow to make this huge jump."

"I invited everyone, Edie, to use this hill. Is it true that the hill is too icy for the youngest ones?"

Edie looked away from Uncle Sol's gaze. "Nooooo, I guess it isn't really icy," she finally acknowledged.

"Do I mind if the boys build jumps and make some holes in the snow?" Uncle Sol questioned further.

"Noooo … but you should!" Edie shot back.

Uncle Sol just looked at Edie. All of a sudden she realized she was being very selfish—and very wrong. Edie looked away and swallowed hard to get rid of the lump that was growing in her throat. Nobody in the neighborhood ever wanted to disappoint Uncle Sol for any reason.

"I chose you to be the 'protector' this year, didn't I?" Uncle Sol continued.

"Yes, but it's not as much fun as I thought it was going to be," Edie confided.

"I know. There are times when it isn't much fun, Edie. I chose you because I believed, and I still believe, you are old enough to handle the important responsibility of protecting the younger children. But, I didn't choose you to give you more privileges than everyone else."

Edie became aware of how quiet it was in the backyard. She heard the unmistakable change in the tone of Uncle Sol's voice as he said gently, "Edie, it's my hill and it's my yard. I want everybody to enjoy it. Everybody, including you." Edie nodded that she understood.

THE SLIDING HILL / 97

"Now, as 'protector' for this season—I'm assuming you will still be the 'protector'?" Uncle Sol looked at Edie with raised eyebrows as he interrupted himself to see if she was still willing, even after being corrected.

"If you'll still have me," Edie said quietly.

"Of course, I'll still have you. This is on-the-job-training. Now, what do you need to do right this minute?"

"I need to get all the kids who are out front and invite them in."

"And?"

"And tell them I'm sorry for what I've done to them today. Is there anything else?" Edie asked.

"Just one more thing," Uncle Sol added with a twinkle in his eye. When you get back here with the others, you and I will have a race down the hill. I want to see if I can top that last run you had!"

Acts 10: 34f

Theological Foundation: see p.207
Guide for Non-religious Settings: see p.247

Patina Sisters

"I have the most rotten sisters on the planet!" Will wailed as he ran up the street away from his house. Will was not having a good day. In fact, he was pretty angry with his sisters. All day long they kept bothering him … coming into his room … asking to play with the electronic game he had gotten for his birthday not that long ago. All Will wanted was to be left alone in his room so he could play by himself. But his sisters were very persistent. They kept trying to come into his room even when Will had locked the door. Unfortunately, Will had taught his sisters how to unlock bedroom doors with an unbent paper clip when they had accidentally locked themselves out of their room, so they knew how to get into his room even when he locked it to keep them out.

"Get out of my room!" Will leaped up from his bed and chased the giggling girls out the door and down the stairs, "And stay out … just wait till I tell Mom!" He lumbered back up the stairs, carefully locked his bedroom door, settled down on the bed and began playing the game again. Within minutes there was the distinctive click that meant the girls had unlocked the door again. They burst into the room and leaped on the bed trying to grab the game from Will. "Get out of my room!" he bellowed again and the chase was on. So that is how it went … over and over again the girls repeated the game of their own. Their mother had gone to the store and the girls took full advantage of the situation. Not one of them heard their mother return from the store, but that's when things went from bad to worse for Will. "Get out of my rooms you monsters!" He yelled as he chased them downstairs. And that is when their mother came out of the kitchen.

"What is going on, girls?" their mother asked as they hid behind her with well-practiced "fear" showing on their faces as they looked at their brother. Will was standing in the hallway glaring at the girls behind his mother and trying to control himself.

"Mom, Will won't let us come in his room. He keeps locking the door and playing that game. He won't share it and besides, he's been playing the game the whole time you were at the store."

"Mom, they kept breaking into my room. I asked them to leave and they wouldn't and then they tried to take my game away ... you know, the one you and Dad gave me. They are being ridiculous! Don't listen to them."

"Have you been playing that the whole time I was at the store?"

"Yes he was Mom, the minute you left..."

Will wanted to deny it, but he couldn't. He just shot his two sisters the "I-can't-stand-you-and-you're-going-to-get-it-when-I-get-a-chance" look.

"Will, you know the rules your father and I set up about this game. I want it down here in the kitchen with me right now. You have played all you are going to play today. As for your bedroom door, I've told you not to lock it many times. Perhaps we need to change the door knob so this won't be an issue."

That had been the last straw. Will just put on his coat and took off down the street. He kicked every rock he found on the street and he kicked one so hard that it ricocheted off Uncle Sol's fence not far from where his neighbor was sweeping the walkway that went to the backyard.

"Hey, Will, that was a pretty strong kick..."

"Yeah, well I wish I could kick my sisters; I can't stand them!"

And because Uncle Sol was just standing there looking like he would listen, Will blurted out everything that had just happened and how awful his sisters were.

"My mother says I'm supposed to love my sisters and I'm supposed to forgive them, but I can't *stand* them. They are so *rotten*. They always mess my things up and they always gang up on me. And I'm supposed to forgive them? I bet even God doesn't want to forgive my sisters. They are *so* mean!"

It got very quiet. Will was aware of birds singing and the crack of a baseball on a bat from the pick-up game being played down the block. Uncle Sol just looked at Will and then quite unexpectedly, he smiled.

"What are you smiling at, Uncle Sol?" Will said grumpily.

"I was just remembering something."

"What?"

"Well, I know that your dad and you like to make things out of wood and you're pretty good at it. And I seem to remember last time I visited your house I saw a table your grandfather made. I was just wondering … if that table had a scratch on it, would you throw it away?"

Will was annoyed at Uncle Sol for changing the subject, but he went along with him. "Why would we? A scratch isn't going to wreck a table. It's still beautiful and it's still works for us. I mean a scratch isn't going to keep me from eating dinner at the table … What has that got to do with my sisters, anyway?"

Uncle Sol persisted with his own thought, "If you dented the tool box you made with your dad, would you get rid of that?"

Will was very proud of his tool box. It was the first big project he'd made out of wood and with his dad's help it had turned out beautifully. "Of course not; I don't want it dented, but even if it did get nicked or something, it still holds my tools. It's still a good tool box."

"You have spoken like a true woodworker, Will. And you sound a lot like God."

Will was exasperated and he wasn't sure he'd actually heard Uncle Sol correctly.

"What?"

"No, I mean it, Will. You know God made each and every one of us and he still thinks we are very special and valuable even when we don't do the right things. He isn't willing to throw *us* away either."

Just then Will's sisters walked up the sidewalk and stopped at Uncle Sol's yard where the older and younger neighbors were talking. "We're sorry, Will. We were being pests. Mom was pretty mad at us after she found out how much we were bugging you the whole time she was shopping. Will you forgive us, Will?"

"Why would I...," Will started to protest and then he looked at Uncle Sol who quietly stood by tapping the wooden handle on his broom.

Will sighed and then sort of smiled. "Yeah, I guess so ... let's go play on the swings in Uncle Sol's backyard. Is that okay, Uncle Sol?"

Uncle Sol smiled, stepped aside and waved them into the backyard.

Psalm 25:1-9

Theological Foundation: see p.209

An Energetic Word

Jenny sat in a notch way above the ground in the tallest ash tree in the neighborhood. It was very convenient that the tree just happened to be growing in the empty lot next to her house. She'd wanted to climb right to the top of that tree ever since she had seen Rocky sitting high above the ground last year yelling his greetings to people up and down the street. The view was spectacular. Jenny could see over the roofs of all the homes, even past Alice's house to the lake and Mr. Koth's farm. She remembered her father saying to her before he was deployed with the National Guard, "Now Jenny, I know how much you love to climb trees, but while I'm away, I'm asking you to stay out of them. It really worries your mother when you get up so high. I think she'll have enough to worry about without adding that one."

"But Daddy, I'm really good at climbing and I'm careful. You *know* that!" Jenny remembered protesting. "I know you are and you know you are, but your mother doesn't know you are ... and ... well, I'm just trying to make things easier for her while I'm away. I'm counting on you to help me do that, okay?"

Jenny remembered agreeing to help make her mother's life easier while her father was away, but somehow she found herself up in this great tree anyway. She could see so much. She could see her friends playing catch and riding their bikes. "Wow, they look so small from way up here," she thought to herself. "I'll just sit up here and watch what they're doing. I am sure they'll never even notice me up this high."

As she was enjoying this bird's eye view of the neighborhood, she noticed Helen wandering down the street quite far from her yard. Helen was Edie's little sister and she was still too young to be allowed to wander around without a big sister or brother watching her. Jenny looked to see if Edie or her brother, Paul were anywhere near. No one seemed to be caring for the wandering child. "Oh, no! There's a car coming and Helen's moving right toward the street!" Jenny thought with alarm. Jenny decided she'd better try to help the little girl even from the great distance up in the treetop and even if she was discovered. Jenny yelled as loudly as she could,

"Stop! Helen, Stop! Go find your mother!"

At that very moment, the strangest thing happened. As soon as Jenny's words hit the air, they took shape. They looked just like Jenny. Her warning word to Helen was even dressed in the same clothes that Jenny had put on that morning! Down the tree her warning word scampered. Once it had reached the ground, it took off running. It ran down the street toward Helen, all the time yelling, "Stop! Helen, stop! Go find your mother!" When her warning word reached the little girl, it took Helen by the hand and led her toward the house where the little girl's mother was just coming out the door calling Helen's name. The word of warning let go of the little girl's hand and raced back down the street into the empty lot and scrambled up the tree as quick as a monkey. When it reached the notch where Jenny was sitting, her word of warning took one hop, landed right back on Jenny's lips and then disappeared. Jenny thought that was a little odd, but she smiled and settled back against the slender tree branches feeling very relieved that Helen was safely back home with her mother.

All of a sudden, Jenny felt a cool breeze slip across her and everything became darker. She looked up and saw that a rather large grayish cloud had covered the sun's smiling face. Then she saw more and more clouds lining up to dash in front of the sun. It really looked as though the clouds were gathering to create a huge thundershower.

"Oh no, not clouds!" she complained to the tree. "We're supposed to have a picnic at Uncle Sol's this evening. Everyone in the whole neighborhood is gonna be there. It just can't rain! If we don't have the picnic today, we'll have to wait another whole week before we can try again."

That's when Jenny started to sing, "Rain, rain, go away, come again another day." And then that strange thing happened again. As soon as her words hit the air, they took shape again. They looked just like Jenny again—even wearing the same clothing she'd put on that morning—again. Only this time her word of command ran through the sky all the way up to the clouds. Jenny's word began pushing the clouds away. It walked right up to the biggest, darkest cloud and began to push against it. Slowly, the cloud began to move and Jenny's word pushed the great dark cloud until it slid all the way out past the horizon. As soon as her word ran back, it piled all the other smaller gray clouds into a giant stack. Jenny's word bent down and after picking up the stack of clouds, carried it to the edge of the horizon where the other cloud had been pushed. Her word opened up its arms and dropped the stack beyond sight. Jenny's word worked until the sky was clear blue again with bright sunshine spilling all over the neighborhood and beyond, as far as Jenny could see. As soon as the last cloud disappeared from the sky, Jenny's word raced back to her, climbed the tree and popped right back into her mouth.

Jenny was quite pleased at having rescued the picnic from a potential wash-out and as she settled back into the comfort of the notch in the ash tree, she began to wonder whether or not every time she opened her mouth and spoke her words would come to life and race off to do whatever it was she had said.

"Just think of all the good things I could do if I just spoke and my word would go do it quick like that." Jenny smiled at the possibilities. But then an awful thought came to her: "Suppose I said something terrible? Suppose when I was mad at my brother or my mother I said something mean and my word went and did it? That would be awful, especially if it's somebody I love." That thought worried Jenny a lot. "Maybe I better not say anything bad to anyone. I mean, it could be terrible and I couldn't live with myself,"Jenny concluded. As she enjoyed the view from her perch high above the neighborhood a new thought entered her mind. "Even if I only say good things and my words only do good things, I'm not gonna be able to explain why there are two of me. Hmmmm ... maybe I'd better not talk until I can figure out how to explain all this." This solution pleased Jenny for the moment so she leaned back against the tree and closed her eyes. The warm sun and the gentle swaying of the tree branches in the breeze were heavenly.

"Jenny, Jenny, wake up, it's time for the picnic!" Jenny opened her eyes. For a moment she didn't know where she was. She had been sitting at the top of the ash tree looking over the neighborhood and suddenly she was looking up into the faces of her two good friends, Jon and Edie.

"How did you guys get up here?" Jenny asked sleepily. Her groggy mind couldn't understand how these friends climbed up in the tree without her noticing.

"Up where, Jenny?" Jon asked.

"Jenny, you were sleeping, you silly," Edie laughed at Jenny's surprised look. "Look, you're right here in the hammock ... in your own yard. It's Saturday afternoon and it's time for the picnic at Uncle Sol's. Come on, get up, you Sleepyhead!"

Jenny rolled to the edge of the hammock and eased herself to the ground. Once her feet touched the grass and she stood up, her friends started to run ahead. "Jenny, come on! We don't have all day!" In their eagerness to get to the picnic they had no patience for their sleepy friend to fully wake up. Jenny stumbled along following behind the two, shaking her head, still trying to wake up, and still trying to make sense of what had just happened.

When she walked through the garden gate at Uncle Sol's, the picnic was in full swing. People were laughing and talking. The other children were playing statue tag out behind the swing set and the sand box.

"Hey, Jenny! How are ya?" one friend after another asked. Jenny would smile and nod, but she didn't open her mouth.

"Wanna come play tag?" another called out to her. Jenny just shook her head "no" and found a chair to sit in where she could just watch all the activity.

"Jenny, would you like something to drink? I've got some lemonade and there are sodas in the cooler." Jenny just shook her head "no" at Uncle Sol's offer.

Uncle Sol looked closely at the solemn girl. "Jenny, are you all right? You haven't spoken a word since you got here."

Jenny nodded her head and shrugged her shoulders trying to say with that quick gesture, "I'm fine, but I don't want to talk. Maybe you could just leave me alone for now, but thanks for asking, okay?"

"Jenny?" Uncle Sol's raised eyebrows showed his concern without ever saying out loud, "Is there anything I can do?" Jenny knew what Uncle Sol was asking by just saying her name that way and she shook her head "no", trying to say to him without words, "I don't need anything."

Uncle Sol sighed, but honored Jenny's wish to be left alone. He joined the other neighbors, but his eyes kept straying back to the chair where she was curled up. Jenny knew he was looking out for her ... and now that she was more fully awake, she really did want to join her friends, but she was frightened. "What if my words do take shape and can really do things? I mean, how would I explain it?" she worried.

Uncle Sol made his way back over to where the girl sat. "Hey, Jenny how about something to eat?" Jenny just shook her head "no" again, but then she saw her older friend's concern spill from his heart right through his eyes reaching out to her.

She finally spoke, "Uncle Sol...?" He sat right down in the chair next to her and Jenny smiled. Her word did not spring out of her mouth and begin to run around. The girl began to laugh. "It was just a dream, Uncle Sol! It was all just a dream! Oh, I was being so silly, but it was so real! Have you ever had a dream that seemed so real, you couldn't be sure that it wasn't?"

"I think we all have at some time or another, Jenny. So tell me, what was this dream? It must have really been scary to keep you silent for so long."

"Well, it wasn't really scary ... not exactly. I mean, it was only scary if it was true and I wasn't sure. I really wasn't sure." Jenny then went on to relate to Uncle Sol the whole dream about being in the tree and all the things her words did.

"Isn't that strange, Uncle Sol? I mean my words looked just like me. When they left my mouth they did exactly what I had said and then they came back to me when they were done. I really was afraid to speak in case it was true 'cause I didn't know how in the world I could explain it."

"Well, that was a strange dream, but it reminds me of so many things I've read in the Bible. In those ancient days people believed that words had a power and life all their own so they were very careful with what they said to each other. And of course, when God spoke, his word created the universe ... and God's Word took the shape of Jesus. And Jesus said that if we saw Him, we were seeing God because Jesus was the Word of God in human shape ... just like your dream where your words took on your shape and did exactly what you said. So, strange as your dream was, the people in Bible times would understand it perfectly."

Jenny took a deep breath and let out a long sigh of relief, "Thank you, Uncle Sol ... thanks for listening. I can't tell you how relieved I am that I really didn't climb the ash tree, because I promised Daddy I wouldn't do that while he's away. You know, I'm glad it's only God's Word that comes to life. It would just be too scary if ours did! Can you imagine how crazy that would be to have us and our words running all over the place?"

"That's a very interesting thought, Jenny. I'm afraid I *can* imagine it!" Uncle Sol said with a laugh. "Like right now, at this picnic ... now that *would* be a sight!"

Jenny smiled, got up from the chair and joined her friends excitedly telling them all about her very strange dream.

John 1:1-18

Theological Foundation: see p.211

The Borrowed Easter Egg

The *Neighborhood Easter Egg Hunt* was a sure sign that winter was past and spring was here to stay. How *The Hunt* had gotten started was a hazy memory, but the traditions surrounding it had not changed in all its long years of existence. The four requirements for *The Hunt* were memorized by every new group of kids as they grew up in the neighborhood:

Number One: every child in the neighborhood is welcome;

Number Two: there is a non-negotiable entry fee of six brightly colored EasterEggs—no plain white or brown eggs allowed;

Number Three: a prize is given to each child as soon as they collect 6 eggs; and

Number Four: a rubber chicken is given to the finder of the last Easter egg. That finder has to keep the rubber chicken for the entire year and display it somewhere prominently in their front yard.

Nobody really wanted to be the one to find the last egg because nobody wanted to display the rubber chicken for a whole year, but it was tradition, after all, so everyone played along. Each year the excitement would build during the 40 days of Lent as Uncle Sol prepared his yard for the annual event. The children would bring their eggs over to Uncle Sol's house right after church on Easter Sunday. Most of the parents would help hide the eggs in Uncle Sol's backyard while the remaining parents would lead the children in games across the street in David's front yard.

When all the eggs had been hidden, Uncle Sol would always walk around to his front yard where the huge old lilac bush grew. In its branches hung his favorite wind chimes. He

would give the branches of the lilac such a shaking that the wind chimes sounded like someone had just spilled musical notes down a flight of stairs. Of course, the egg-seekers would be waiting for just such a commotion and they would come running with their baskets in hand to begin *The Hunt*. As the search would get underway, Uncle Sol would always call out from his deck, "Look carefully—look quickly—You don't want to be the finder of the last egg!"

Well, this year, Will was in trouble. He had insisted on doing his Easter eggs all by himself from the boiling to the coloring.

"Mom, I'm old enough to do my own eggs," he had boldly stated. "I know how to boil them and cool them and color them and I just want to do it myself without any help."

"All right, Will, I'll leave your six eggs here in the bowl in the refrigerator, but your sisters want to do theirs now and they need my help. I'll leave the egg dye in the cups on the kitchen table, but I want them done before dinner and everything cleaned up, too!"

"No problem, Mom. I'll get them done in plenty of time." That's what he had told her, but he hadn't gotten started until late in the afternoon and his mother and father had gone out for an early dinner and a movie, leaving Will and his sisters in the care of their babysitter, Lenora. When he had finally gotten around to boiling his eggs, one had cracked so badly that he just couldn't use it. He had looked in the refrigerator: no eggs left ... absolutely none. "What am I gonna do? I've got to have six colored Easter eggs and I've only got five."

"Will can't do the Easter Egg Hunt, Will can't do the Easter Hunt," his sisters taunted.

"Be quiet! I'll think of something," Will answered angrily as he stomped out the door. With his parents gone, a babysitter without a car, and no eggs—brown or white—left in the house, the boy was stuck. He didn't want to go to any of his friends' houses to borrow an egg because he was sure his mom would just look at him with that, "see, you should have let me help you," look that he hated. Suddenly he realized where he could borrow an egg for a day without anyone finding out about it.

"Hey, Lenora, I'm going to Alice's house at the end of the street. I won't be gone long." Lenora was used to Will hopping on his bike and riding around the neighborhood. His parents had given the babysitter permission to let the boy visit friends on the street so long as he told her where he was going.

"How long ya' gonna be gone?" the teenager asked as she followed him to the garage.

"Maybe half an hour, no more than that."

"Okay, I'll warm up what your mom left for dinner. Be sure you're back here in half an hour."

"Okay, okay, don't worry." Will popped on his helmet, then jumped on his bike and rode as fast as he could to his friend's house. Right across the street from Alice's home by the lake was an old man named Mr. Koth. His property was the real "end" of the neighborhood and all the kids thought of him as a farmer because he had chickens and a few sheep. Mr. Koth had fenced in a field that had more trees than grass in it. His sheep wandered freely about, nibbling bits of green here and there while his flock of chickens poked and scratched the ground in search of seeds. Near the fence on the side of the field closest to the lake, the old man had built a small wooden shed that doubled for a sheep shelter and a hen house. Like Uncle Sol, Mr. Koth was comfortable with the neighborhood kids coming and going on his property. He'd left a clear path between the lake and his pasture for everyone to use. He just wanted the children to be respectful of his land and his animals.

When Will reached Alice's house, he kept going. He didn't stop until he was on the path to the lake. After hiding his bike under some bushes, he began walking quietly along Mr. Koth's pasture fence. "Now, Mr. Koth has always let me come on his property. So I'm gonna just walk on his land and check to see if any of his chickens have eggs. I'll only borrow one and then I'll bring it back after *The Hunt* is over." Will said this out loud softly as if to convince himself what he was doing was okay. When he was across from the wooden shed, Will slipped between the fence rails and crept over to the door.

"Be quiet, Will. No fast moves. You don't need the chickens squawking," he told himself as he lifted the latch. It was very nearly dark inside the little room. Roosting hens clucked as he entered and one stood up looking for food. Ever so slowly, Will moved toward the nest where the hen had been sitting. There were four white eggs bright as they could be. "I'm only gonna borrow one egg, just one. I promise to bring it back," he told the hen. With one swift move, Will scooped up a single white egg and slipped it into his jacket pocket he'd stuffed with some napkins from the kitchen table. Slowly he backed away from the nest and the chicken and found the door. Carefully, he let himself out of the hen house, fastened the latch and made his way through the fence.

Will shouldn't have done it. He knew that what he was doing was wrong, but he wanted to be in *The Hunt* so badly and he didn't want his mom to know that he had not quite handled the job he'd insisted he could do without her help. "Besides," he kept telling himself, "I'm just borrowing it for a few hours." He put his helmet back on and quickly rode his bike home.

"I'm back, Lenora," Will shouted as he ran up the stairs to his room. Within minutes the fresh white egg was brightly colored with washable felt tip markers from his art set. Will was sure none of the other children would put yellow chicks in a wavy design on their eggs. That way he could be sure to claim it after *The Hunt*, wash it off and then sneak back to Mr. Koth's chicken coop to return it.

"Time for dinner, Will," Lenora called from the bottom of the stairs.

"Okay, I'm comin', I'm comin'. I told you I'd be back in plenty of time," he said to Lenora as he walked into the kitchen. He slipped the new egg into his basket.

"Will's not goin' to the Easter Egg Hunt, Will's not goin' to the Easter Egg Hunt." His little sisters started with their singsong taunting again as soon as they came to the dinner table.

"Oh yeah? Count the eggs in my basket," Will ordered.

"Hey, where'd ya' get the other egg?"

"Did Alice give it to you?"

"I got friends in the neighborhood, y'know," Will answered concentrating on his next forkful of food.

Will was uncommonly helpful to Lenora that night. He even helped clean up the kitchen after dinner. Without thinking, he pushed his basket of colored eggs to the back of the table very near the radiator when he wiped off the crumbs left from dinner. The steady heat from the radiator kept the eggs warm all night long.

After attending church with his family, Will joined all the other children in the neighborhood for the *Neighborhood Easter Egg Hunt*. He walked into Uncle Sol's yard with his basket of six eggs just like everyone else. "I hope nobody notices that one of mine has marker on it instead of the regular dye and I hope the parents are really careful when they hide it," he worried as he left his basket on the table with all the others. It wasn't long before one of the parents brought the empty baskets around to David's yard. The games stopped and everyone found his or her basket and just stood waiting for the wind chimes. When the loud ringing filled the air, the kids broke into a run. Will was the first one to enter the garden.

"I've just got to find Mr. Koth's egg right away," he thought as he searched under bushes and behind trees and flowers. Alice was finding eggs, so was Edie, so were Jon and Julie, too. Everybody was finding eggs all over the garden; Will began to get frantic. He was trying to look for eggs while at the same time trying to check each kid's basket to see if his egg had been found so that he could trade for it. He was trying to not make it obvious that he was inspecting everyone's findings. Nobody had yet found Mr. Koth's egg.

"I've got my six," one child called out.

"Come over and get your prize," Uncle Sol called out over the din of excited chatter. "I've got my six," joined in another, and another. Even Will had found six eggs. One of the well established rules for *The Hunt* was that once a child had found six eggs and collected the prize from Uncle Sol, he or she was to help younger children who were still looking.

"You're getting warmer ... warmer ... oh, you're going to burn your hand if you get any closer!" Edie hinted to Helen who still didn't have her six eggs. Helen squealed with delight as she spotted the deep purple egg under the tulip leaves. The little girl ran as fast as she could to Uncle Sol to collect her prize.

"We have only one egg left," Uncle Sol called out over the happy chatter. "Come on now, everyone: look hard. I don't want to find it three weeks from now!" Jon, with only five eggs in his own basket, had already spotted his sixth egg. It was completely hidden by ferns and he had just caught a glimpse of the bright yellow decorations on its side, but he was in no hurry to pick it up. Anytime a child wandered near the ferns he simply said, "I already checked there." When Will asked, he assured him that no eggs were left in that area. Jon wanted that rubber chicken. He'd listened to his sister tell everyone how much she hated that chicken and how disgusted she would be to have to look at it every day. That was incentive enough for Jon. He had to be the last one to find the sixth egg.

Will was scrambling to find that egg because the last egg just happened to be Mr. Koth's egg. Minutes passed as heads bobbed everywhere in the garden. Someone was going to get the silly chicken for finding that last egg.

All of a sudden, when Jon figured the wait had been long enough, he yelled, "I found it! I found it!" His delight at hearing Uncle Sol announce, "Jon is the winner of the rubber chicken," and his sister's anguished groan, "Oh no! Not a year of that ugly chicken in our yard!" quickly shifted to surprise as he looked more closely at his egg. "Hey ... look ... it's breaking open!" All the kids rushed to where Jon knelt holding an egg that was rocking back and forth in his hand. Sure enough, the egg was breaking.

"Uncle Sol, look, I can see a beak breaking through the shell! Look, it's trying to peck its way out."

Uncle Sol hurried across the grass to join Jon and the others. Even the parents gathered around to watch the birth of a chick. "Well, where did this egg come from?" asked Uncle Sol. Will wanted to melt away. He wanted a hole to open up right beneath his feet so he'd just disappear. He hoped his face was not giving away his secret. He was practically holding his breath, he was so nervous that he'd be discovered right here in front of all these people.

The little chick continued to peck an opening in the shell. Uncle Sol finally broke the hush that had come over the Easter egg hunters as they continued to watch the chick's progress.

"This is wonderful—to have a real example of Easter right here in Jon's hand. Do any of you know why we even *have* Easter Eggs?"

"To give *you* a reason to do your spring yard work and *us* a reason to rummage through your yard?" one parent joked.

"Well...," Uncle Sol pretended like that might be the answer, but then he said, "no seriously, do any of you know why we have eggs on Easter?" Now the older neighbor was looking at all the kids. Everyone shook his or her head 'no,' so Uncle Sol went on

"On Easter, as you know, Jesus rose from the dead and ever after people have tried to find a way to show how wonderful a miracle it is—from death to life. Just like this egg. It looked dead, like all these other eggs, but really—as you can now see—there was life inside all along and ... look: this little one is finally breaking free of the shell just the way Jesus broke free of death and came out of the tomb on that first Easter." All the kids crowded around to get a better look—all except Will.

Uncle Sol, who seemed to notice everything, asked, "Will does this egg belong to you by any chance?" Will looked at the ground. All eyes turned to look at him. This was it; there was no escape for Will now. His eyes started to sting a bit as he said, "Well, I brought it, but it doesn't exactly belong to me ... it belongs to Mr. Koth." Will gulped and hurried on, "I just borrowed it from one of his hens because I only had five eggs and my parents were gone last night and I didn't want to miss *The Hunt* today. I was planning on returning it as soon as we were finished, but I couldn't find it..." Will's voice trailed off.

"Well, I think you'd better take this little chick home to its mother so it can have a happy Easter, too." Uncle Sol said as he gently guided Jon in handing over the hatching chick, shell and all, to Will.

Will cradled the hatching chick in his hands and began walking out of the yard. He carefully carried the chick back to Mr. Koth's house with a parade of neighborhood kids behind him. Mr. Koth came outside when he heard all the noise coming up his drive way. He was very surprised to see a hatching chick in Will's hand. After the boy handed the wriggling, damp baby bird and its shell to Mr. Koth, he explained why he had it and apologized for borrowing without asking.

"Mr. Koth, if you'll let me, I'll come over and clean out your hen house next time it needs it." The kids all looked at each other in amazement at Will's offer. Even fifty feet away from the lake path, the smells of the hen house often made them hold their breaths and hurry past it. Many noses wrinkled at the thought of actually standing inside and cleaning out the mess.

"Well, that's quite an offer, Will. I hate that job, myself." Mr. Koth thought for a moment: with all these kids around it might be good for Will to have to pay some consequence for his action, even though no real harm had been done.

"Okay—I think that's a fair exchange for borrowing my egg without asking. Sure, I'll let you do that—and thanks for returning my chick," he said. The old man watched the chick trying to stand up for the first time, then he smiled and said, "Come on, chick, it's time to meet your mama."

As the children returned to Uncle Sol's house, Jon turned to Will, "Will, that was really dumb to borrow an egg from Mr. Koth's chicken, but I'm kinda glad you did. I think Uncle Sol made so much sense when he talked about Jesus breaking out of the tomb and the chick breaking out of the egg."

"I think it'd be great if we could have a live chick hatching every Easter, just to remind us," Alice chimed in since she was walking next to the two boys and overheard their conversation.

"I'll tell you one thing," Will called out over his shoulder as he started to run, "I won't be bringing the hatching egg!" Jon, Alice and the rest of the neighborhood kids were right at his heels as they all raced up the street toward Uncle Sol's garden.

Mark 16:1ff

Theological Foundation: see p.213

Weed Seeds

Alice enjoyed solitude. She enjoyed people, too, but she found that time alone was not necessarily lonely time. If she had some time to herself, she often went into the field right behind her home to play and explore.

It was a beautiful fall day when Alice found some 'alone time' and waded out into the dry grass until she reached a patch of weeds that were nearly as tall as she was. That's when she saw something she had never noticed before. Just as the breeze began to blow ever so gently, seeds began floating out of a very gnarly-shaped part of a tall plant. When she looked closely, she could see hundreds of seeds inside the graying pod. As the wind blew stronger, more and more seeds tumbled out floating on the wind, almost as if they had sails.

Alice loved seeing how gently they flew and she wanted to share her exciting new discovery with the neighborhood kids. That was when an idea began to form in her mind. The more she thought about it the better she liked it. So right then and there she decided to collect some 'sailing seeds' and share them with all the other kids in the neighborhood. As she gathered seeds from the seedpod, she got another idea. She would not give the seeds to her friends directly; she would surprise them by planting them in their gardens when they weren't looking and then next year they would have 'sailing seeds' plants of their very own.

Well, that's exactly what Alice did. In a single afternoon she filled one of her mother's cloth grocery bags with 'sailing seeds'. The 'sail' was so soft and silky while the seed was hard and smooth. Alice thought the contrast of the white silk and the hard brown seed was particularly pretty. She really wanted to tell her friends and show them all the seeds she'd collected, but then she remembered how wonderful it had been to discover the 'sailing seeds' for herself and she wanted her friends to have the fun of finding out about the wonderful seeds in that same "accidental" way.

Once she had the seeds, she began the next part of her plan. After school, once she had made sure she was all alone and unseen by any of the neighborhood kids, Alice tip-toed into a neighbor's garden. Carefully, she poked several holes in the flower bed with a stick. Next, she dropped some 'sailing seeds' into the holes. Finally, she gently covered up the seeds so that no one would know where she had been or what she had done. It took her several days to plant all the seeds in everyone's flower gardens. Just when she wanted to be alone to carry out her plan, it seemed like all the kids were out in their yards wanting to play. At last, she had only one neighbor left. She had saved the best for last: Uncle Sol.

Uncle Sol had the most beautiful gardens in the neighborhood. No matter what the time of the year, Uncle Sol's garden was wonderful—even in winter. Everyone knew they could find him out in his garden nearly everyday planting, weeding, pruning or just enjoying it. He always wanted to share his garden, too. The neighborhood children knew they were always welcome any time so Alice was sure it would be all right if she brought some of her special "sailing seeds" into Uncle Sol's garden. The hardest part was finding a time when no one was around because she really wanted to surprise Uncle Sol most of all.

Alice watched Uncle Sol work all afternoon planting bulbs right next to his door. Finally, he went inside. That's when Alice decided to act. She sneaked in and poked several holes in the flowerbed where Uncle Sol had been working. Just as she was dropping in the last seeds and was filling the holes with dirt, she heard a yell,

"Uncle Sol … hurry, hurry … Uncle Sol." The door opened and the screen door slammed as Uncle Sol hurried down the steps to the front walk.

"What is it, Edie? What's happened?"

"Uncle Sol, I saw Alice wrecking your flower bed and I knew you had worked so hard planting all those daffodil bulbs. She was poking a stick right there…" Edie pointed to the exact spot where Alice had been working. Uncle Sol turned to Alice with one of those quizzical looks on his face.

"Alice? Is that true? Were you poking my daffodil bulbs with a stick?"

Alice had no idea that anyone had seen her. Now her secret was ruined and her friends actually thought she was trying to do harm to Uncle Sol. With Uncle Sol looking at her and Edie glaring at her, she could feel her lip beginning to tremble. She couldn't speak because she was afraid she would cry and to make matters worse, Edie's loud yelling had attracted most of the neighborhood children. Now it seemed like everyone in the whole world was forming a circle around her and Uncle Sol.

Uncle Sol knelt down closer to Alice.

"Knowing you, Alice, if you did poke holes in my garden, you must have had a good reason."

Alice nodded, knowing she'd have to say something, but now everyone was going to hear. Before she could say a word, Will spoke up.

"I saw Alice out in the field picking seeds from the weeds out there. It looked like she was filling a whole bag full of weed seeds. I wondered what she was doing so I followed her to Jenny's house. She poked a stick in her garden, too, and then she planted some of those weed seeds in the holes. I bet she put weed seeds in your garden, Uncle Sol. She's trying to ruin it."

At last, Alice could talk. "No I wasn't, Uncle Sol! I, I wanted to give you a present of 'sailing seeds'. I thought if I could plant them in your garden you would be surprised next year when you got the 'sailing seeds' right in your yard." Looking around at all the other children she defended herself, "I, I wanted to give them to everyone, just the way Uncle Sol gives us beautiful flowers every year." Everyone started to laugh … and Alice hid her face behind her arm.

"Hold on, hold on…" It was Uncle Sol's turn to speak up.

"I do plant flowers and take care of my gardens so that all of you can enjoy them. I love all of God's creation, but I am especially fond of flowers and gardens." Uncle Sol walked back to the steps leading to his front door and sat down. He motioned for Alice to sit down next to him while the other kids gathered around,

"Listen, ever since I was a little boy, I wanted to say 'thank you' to God for making such a beautiful world by helping plants grow. When I got to be a grown up, I began turning all this land into a gift that I could give back to God."

Uncle Sol took off his ball cap and rubbed his head before he began again,

"I didn't want anyone to hurt the flowers and ruin my gift to God so I wouldn't let anyone in this yard."

Amazed looks darted between all the kids. They had never heard this before and they never could have guessed this about their elder neighbor. Uncle Sol continued, "However, if God had thought that way none of us would ever have lived in this wonderful creation. God shared all the flowers and trees with human beings and the best way for me to say 'thank you, God' to show God I loved him was to share all the flowers and trees with my neighbors … that means all of you, your sisters and brothers, your parents and grandparents. It took me awhile to stop worrying about the grass or the possibility of broken flowers." Uncle Sol chuckled, "Then, one day I suddenly realized that the real flowers in my garden are not the ones in the dirt. No, the real flowers are all of *you*. You are my roses and my daffodils and my tulips. You're the garden I'm tending. I think that was the most important lesson God ever taught me."

Most of the children didn't really understand how they could be Uncle Sol's flowers, but they felt deep down the welcome he extended to each and every one of them, not only into his yard, but into his life.

Uncle Sol turned his attention back to the cause of the impromptu gathering on his front steps. "Alice, that was very kind of you to share—what did you call them? 'Sailing seeds'? Well, it was very kind to share the 'sailing seeds' with us." For the first time, Alice's dejected look began to ease away.

"You're certainly starting out just like I did, but with a huge difference: you're already thinking of others," he said with a gentle smile. "I do have one piece of advice, though. I think it is important to ask before you plant something in someone else's yard. Now I'm going to leave my seeds right where you put them because I can see from the ones still in your bag that while they *are* from weeds, they're not ordinary weeds, they're milkweed. So I'm hoping next year that butterflies will be coming right here to my door step."

Edie piped up, "Do you mean the milkweeds are good for butterflies?"

"That's exactly what I mean. Anything we can do to help butterflies is a good thing," replied Uncle Sol as he got up. "Come on, Alice, I've got a couple other places I'd like to put those 'sailing seeds'."

Alice wiped the back of her hand across her eyes to take away any trace of the tears that had been there. "As soon as I finish planting with Uncle Sol, I'll show all of you where I buried the seeds in your yards in case you want to move them," she said as she walked eagerly toward the backyard with her elder neighbor.

Mark 12:28-34

Theological Foundation: see p.215

Lessons in Freezing

Rocky loved ice fishing more than any other winter activity. During his first year in the neighborhood, Uncle Sol had taught him how to dig holes with a hand ice auger and how to set the traps, which were actually mini versions of fishing poles with flags on them set up over the holes. Once he started catching fish in the lake on the edge of the neighborhood, Rocky was hooked. His enthusiasm had inspired some of the other boys to take up ice fishing, too. Now winter was his favorite season and with the approaching spring weather warming the temperatures day and night, Rocky could see the season of his favorite pastime slipping away. All week long, it had rained and every day after school, Rocky had stopped by Uncle Sol's house.

"What'd y' think, Uncle Sol? Is the season really over? I mean there's still plenty of ice out there on the lake. I've been checking."

"Rocky, I've been doing a little checking myself. There's quite a lot of standing water on the ice. With the warm days and all that water on top of the ice from the rain—and don't forget, there's warmer water under the ice—that ice is weakening every day. If we have many more days like this, we're going to see open water pretty soon."

"Yeah, I know, but don't you think we've got one more weekend?"

"Rocky, I really don't think so. I want you to be safe and all the conditions point to danger. Please don't think any more about going out on the ice. The season's over. Let it go."

"Uncle Sol, it can't be…" Rocky started to protest, but Uncle Sol's raised eyebrows let Rocky know he'd heard Uncle Sol's final warning and the conversation was over.

The next morning, just when everyone had started thinking that spring was right around the corner, Friday dawned cold ... freezing cold. Rocky's heart was soaring.

"Hey, Nick, y' notice how cold it is?"

"How could I miss it, Rocky? I was freezing at the bus stop this morning."

"I know. That's the point. You were freezing. And the puddles were all frozen again and that means the water at the lake is freezing again. Y' wanna go fishin' in the morning?"

"Well...," Nick hesitated

"No 'well', just say 'yes'. I swear it'll be the last time this season we'll get the chance. I checked the weather channel and it's supposed to stay cold all the way 'til Monday."

"Yeah, who wants to miss the last time for the season? Sure, sure, I'll go."

"Hey, what plans am I missing?" Will asked as he overheard the two others talking on the bus ride home.

"We're goin' fishin' in the morning. Y' wanna come? It'll be the last time this season, I'm pretty sure." Rocky's enthusiasm was always contagious.

"I'll be ready," Will answered.

Rocky did not stop by Uncle Sol's house to ask what he thought about ice conditions that afternoon because Rocky was certain the ice would be fine now that it was cold again.

Saturday morning was bright and clear, the wind was cold and all the puddles were still frozen as Rocky walked down to Nick's house. He had the willow splint pack basket on his back filled with ice fishing gear.

"Wow, it's winter again!" Nick said as he fell into step with Rocky.

"Yeah, I love it!" Rocky exclaimed.

Will was watching for his friends from the warmth of his living room.

"I just wish there was a way to go ice fishing and not freeze your fingers and toes off," Will commented as he joined the two teens and shoved his gloved hands into his pockets. Will's enjoyment of ice fishing was based completely on the fact that the two oldest boys in the neighborhood invited him to come along. He never ate the fish they caught, quite happy to send them to Rocky's and Nick's tables for supper. The three boys walked down the quiet street toward the lake. The neighborhood always took its time moving on Saturday mornings, but especially when it was cold.

The boys discovered a thin layer of skim ice on the surface. Since Will was the first to reach the edge of the lake, he was the first to step on the lake's surface—and the ice broke. His boot went right into the water.

"Hey, Rocky," Will gasped, "this doesn't look safe. I mean the lake isn't frozen all the way to the bottom."

"Oh, it's just the edge; it'll be fine. Don't worry!" Nothing was going to keep the eager fisherman from his last day of fishing. "I've seen it just like this before and the ice is just fine when you step out a couple of feet." Rocky was the oldest and Will trusted him—but still…

"Uncle Sol said it was okay, didn't he?"

"Well, last I talked to him, he said if the weather kept getting warmer the season would be over—but it got colder instead so the season isn't over." That answer satisfied Will. After all, Uncle Sol had taught Rocky everything about ice-fishing and Uncle Sol was always careful. Even so, as Will stepped again, the thin ice broke and his boot splashed into water, but this time the solid ice underneath held him up. Will could feel a creeping worry rise inside of him.

"That's stupid, don't be a chicken," he said to himself. He didn't want to be left out, but this was not going to be the carefree walk across the lake that it had been all winter.

Rocky and Nick just laughed at him when Will asked one more time if they should reconsider going fishing. The two older boys started clumping out across the lake to their favorite fishing spot. Step … crack … splash …step … crack … splash. Only after the splash would the boot find the solid ice underneath. The walking was hard. Catching their breath became more important than conversation as the boys made their way across the watery ice.

"I know what happened," Rocky finally said as he stopped to readjust the heavy pack. "The rain just stayed on top of the old ice and then when it got cold again, it didn't have time to freeze all the way down. This is like having an ice sandwich: thin ice, rain water and then thick ice." That made sense to all of them as they looked back at the jagged trail they'd made.

"I'm chewing up the sandwich!" Rocky shouted as he stomped on ahead with Nick and Will following his broken ice trail. Their boots and their pants were getting soaked, but they were working up such a sweat that none of them felt cold.

The creeping worry wasn't creeping anymore; it leaped from Will's stomach right to his throat. The water was definitely getting deeper than when they had first started. It almost came over the top of his boots with each step. In fact, he couldn't be sure, but it almost felt like the second layer of ice was moving, sinking a little under his feet. Just as he thought "We should stop," there was a loud crack and scream as Rocky plunged into the lake. He'd broken right through the top layer and the bottom layer of ice was too thin. In an instant, the ice hole opened up and Nick and Will were both in water, too. The shock of the cold water just astounded them. Will was the closest to the edge. He managed to kick his way back to the submerged ice shelf. Somehow he got himself up on it. It was thick enough to hold him.

"Help! Help!" he screamed. Rocky and Nick were trying to stay afloat. Fortunately, the loose straps on the pack basket allowed it to slip off Rocky's shoulders when he plunged into the water preventing the boy from being dragged to the bottom. The shock of the icy water made their muscles lock and both boys slipped beneath the surface. Even under water, Nick was trying to get to the ice shelf and Will's outstretched hand! Both Rocky and Nick managed to struggle back to the surface and get their heads above water. "Help! Help! Somebody help us!" Will yelled again for help as he lay on the waterlogged ice shelf straining to reach Nick's hand.

None of the boys saw the man moving as quickly as he dared across the ice with a rope and a long pole. But in the midst of all the thrashing and splashing, a familiar voice broke in.

"Grab the pole, Will. Slide it to Nick and hang on to your end." In one swift motion, Uncle Sol slid the pole right to Will's side.

"Rocky! Grab the rope!" Uncle Sol stood back far from the ragged edge of open water and threw the rope to Rocky. Rocky's fingers were so cold he could barely close them around the floating line, but he managed to close his hand over it as he sank beneath the surface again. Uncle Sol pulled and pulled until he had dragged Rocky onto the ice shelf some distance from the other two. The teen lay in the icy water covering the old ice, gasping for air.

Nick was next. He had grabbed hold of the pole Will held out for him, shivering violently as he waited for his turn to be pulled from the water.

"Nick, I'm gonna throw the rope to you, just like I did for Rocky. You're going to have to grab it and then let go of the pole."

"I, I, I cccannn'"tttt, I, I ccccaaannn'"ttt" the terrified boy chattered.

"You've got to, I can't get any closer to the edge with you two boys there or we'll all go in…"

"Cccccooommm ooonnn NNNNick," Will urged, "yyy-oouuuuu ccccannnnn doooooo itttt."

Nick's fingers inched toward the end of the pole where the knotted end of the rope lay partially submerged. In a lunge of desperation he snagged the rope and Uncle Sol pulled the boy to safety.

"Boys, you've got to get up and walk … and we have to space out … we don't want to put too much pressure on the ice as we go back." The boys were trembling uncontrollably as they stumbled single file toward the shore in their waterlogged clothes with Uncle Sol following behind them.

"Come on, boys ... you're doing great ... just keep moving ... that's it ... just keep moving. There's a warm van waiting for you ... you can see it, can't you? Okay, you're gonna be fine, just put one foot in front of the other ... it won't take long ... I'll even let you listen to your radio station when we get in..."

That last statement brought a trace of a smile to Rocky's face. He knew how much Uncle Sol disliked his music. "All right, we're almost there ... I've got some blankets I'm going to put around you ... just huddle together, okay?" Uncle Sol helped the boys into the back seat and covered them as best he could. Then he turned up the heat to 'high' and directed it all at the boys' faces and feet. The noise of chattering teeth was the only sound to be heard from the back seat. No one asked for music. In fact, no one talked at all as the older neighbor drove the three boys to the hospital.

Uncle Sol called the boys' homes the moment they reached the emergency room. Mothers, fathers and grandparents scrambled to their children's sides. They thanked Uncle Sol as they held their 'thawing out' sons and wouldn't let them go. The fright of how close they'd come to tragedy pushed the sterner questions aside for later.

The boys were finally allowed to go home late in the day after they were thoroughly warmed and the medical staff was convinced there would be no lasting effects of the ice water baths the boys had taken.

"Mom, could we stop by Uncle Sol's on the way home?" Rocky asked. "I need to thank him, and uhhh, I need to get an answer to a question that's been buggin' all of us."

"Sure, I think I might like to just thank him again myself," Rocky's mother said.

"Maybe you could call him instead, Mom? Could ya' just wait in the car for me? It'll only be a minute." Rocky gave his mother that 'I need to do this alone' look.

"Yes, of course I could," his mother said, taking the hint. As his mother pulled into Uncle Sol's driveway, two other cars followed. Three car doors opened and three boys spilled out.

"Rocky ... Nick ... Will...," Uncle Sol opened his door and held out his arms to embrace the boys. Rocky threw his arms around his rescuer and gave him a big bear hug before stepping back to let the other boys have their turns.

"Uncle Sol, I guess I'm the spokesman. We've all had this question just going through our heads all day at the hospital and we gotta have an answer before we go home. How did y'know to come? I mean how did y'know? Do you realize if you hadn't been there ... well, if you hadn't been there...," Rocky couldn't say anymore.

Uncle Sol took a deep breath as he motioned for the boys to come gather close around the warm fire. "Well, this morning, for some reason, I got up a little earlier than usual. When I went out to get the newspaper, I saw you boys down at the end of the street near the path to the lake. Because of the conversation I'd had with you on Thursday, Rocky, about the ice being too dangerous for any more ice fishing, I figured you were just going for an early hike."

Rocky hung his head, but kept listening.

"But after I started reading the paper, I just got this nagging feeling that just wouldn't leave me alone. It dawned on me you might think the cold snap would make it okay to go back out on the lake and I decided I'd better go check. You know I always carry a rope and blankets in the van in the winter and I tossed the pole in just in case. I really wasn't planning on having to use any of it."

The boys tightened the circle around their rescuer as they realized Uncle Sol's willingness to act on that nudge was the only thing that had saved them.

"I've tried to tell you about the dangers, but I knew you really weren't listening. Well, that's not true—I think you actually *were* listening, you just didn't like what I said. You just had no idea how dangerous it could be to ignore what I was trying to tell you."

Uncle Sol let out his breath slowly in a big sigh, "I just wanted to spare you this lesson. I'm so grateful you are all alive."

"Uncle Sol, I'm so grateful for you," Rocky said hoarsely. Nick and Will just nodded their heads in agreement.

"I'm sure I don't need to add another lecture to what you've already gotten today, do I?" The boys shook their heads "no". They'd had quite enough lessons for one day.

Luke 13:31-35

Theological Foundation: see p.217
Guide for Non-religious Settings: see p.248

The Christmas Star

David did not know what to say. He didn't know how he was supposed to act. He'd never had anyone he knew die before. He didn't like what he was feeling inside. First, it felt like someone gave him too many dry crackers to eat because he couldn't swallow. Then it felt like someone took all the bones out of his legs because he felt like he couldn't stand up very well. Then it felt like his eyes were full of sand from crying so much. He was all jumbled up inside and he knew it. Ever since his mother had told him that his Grandpa had died and gone to be with God and grandma, he hadn't felt like himself at all.

They had left their home in a hurry to go to the farmhouse where his grandfather had lived. David missed the Christmas pageant practice at church. He missed the party at school and he missed the neighborhood Christmas party with all his friends at Uncle Sol's house. But mostly he missed his grandfather.

David loved his grandfather very much. His grandfather had lived alone for many years and had always invited David to spend time on the farm in the summer. He had taught David how to fish and how to track animals in the woods. He had trusted David with a hatchet long before anyone back at home would let David touch anything sharp. Together, they had worked on the woodpile and gotten things all ready for Grandpa's house in the winter. David had learned to carve wood with his grandfather and even had his own pocketknife that his grandfather had kept in a special drawer just for David's visits. He was not sure how he could live or even breathe without his grandfather.

And now here it was just four days before Christmas. David wandered out in his yard poking a stick into the snow just to see how deep it was. He really didn't feel like playing or being with anyone so he just kept his head down poking at the snow.

"Hey, David, I am very sorry to hear about your grandfather." Uncle Sol was filling his birdfeeders in his backyard when he saw David. The boy just nodded his head so Uncle Sol would know that he had heard him talking. Uncle Sol finished with the last feeder and quietly went back inside his house. Then David started thinking ... maybe Uncle Sol would be the right one to ask the question that had been burning up inside of him for days now. Uncle Sol seemed to know everything about everything. Uncle Sol wouldn't think he was crazy or something. David poked a few more holes in the snow and then he did it. He just did it. He walked over to Uncle Sol's house and knocked on his door.

"Come in, David," Uncle Sol motioned David to take a seat on the stool in his kitchen. "I was just pouring myself some hot chocolate. Want some?" David shook his head, "no."

"I actually wanted to ask you something, Uncle Sol. Well I really wanted to tell you something. Well ... maybe I want to tell you something and then ask you something."

"I'm ready, David".

"You know how my grandpa died and we went to his farmhouse. Well, when I walked into his house with all my family, I just couldn't stay in there. I mean everywhere I looked I kept thinking I would see Grandpa, but I didn't. I couldn't stand being there, so I just ran outside. I didn't even put a jacket on. It was so dark and cold, but I just ran and ran until I got down to the pond where Grandpa and I used to fish. It was all frozen and covered with snow. I just stood there and shivered and I was sort of, well, I was crying. I was really mad at God and I just stood there at the edge of the pond and I yelled up to God in heaven. I said, 'God, what did you do with my Grandpa? Where is he?' Just as I said that,

Uncle Sol, the very minute the words left my mouth this huge shooting star went across the sky right across my grandpa's house. It was the brightest and longest shooting star I've ever seen. I kept watching for more shooting stars and there wasn't a single one. After the star went by, I didn't feel mad anymore. It seemed like everything was going to be all right." David got very quiet.

"So that is the 'telling' part, David. What's the 'asking' part?" Uncle Sol spoke very softly.

"The 'asking part' is this: do you think God was answering my question about Grandpa with a star?"

"God answers all our prayers, David."

"I wasn't praying, Uncle Sol, I was yelling and I was mad."

"That was still a prayer, David. You were talking to God and he heard you." Uncle Sol paused. In the stillness that rested between the two neighbors, the ticking wall clock seemed particularly loud. After several moments, Uncle Sol gently said, "Tell me again what happened when you saw the star."

"I, I can't explain it, but somehow my insides didn't hurt as much. It was sort of like when you take a really big breath and then let all the air out ... you feel that quiet before you take another breath. That's what it was like. I didn't feel all alone either, even though no one was with me. I just didn't feel alone anymore."

"You were feeling comforted, David. Jesus said, 'Blessed are those who mourn for they shall be comforted.' That's what God was giving you. God speaks to us all the time if we keep our hearts open. We read in the Bible that God often uses people to comfort and guide us. And you know how God used a star so long ago to guide three men to Baby Jesus. So let me ask you, do *you* think God was answering your question, David?"

David was very, very quiet and then he said, "Uncle Sol, I don't know what God has done with my Grandpa, but I know that after I saw the star I didn't feel alone anymore and my heart didn't hurt as much. I think God was letting me know I wasn't alone and I think he was letting me know that my Grandpa is not alone, that God's taking care of him, too."

"David that's the message the star in Bethlehem gave to the whole world. It's the most important message of all time to all people. God said to all of us, 'You are not alone. I am with you' the very moment Jesus was born. And I can tell you this much for sure, David: God won't ever let us walk alone again, not in this life or even when we die. That's a promise Jesus made and it's one he keeps."

David had been looking very intently at the kitchen counter but he suddenly looked up and said, "I was thinking that I didn't even want to celebrate Christmas this year, Uncle Sol, but I've changed my mind. I want God to know that I'm very glad he decided to never leave us alone." Uncle Sol smiled at David and reached over the kitchen counter to tousle the boy's hair.

"I think you've got it, Neighbor. Merry Christmas, David, Merry Christmas."

Matthew 2:1-11
Matthew 5:4

Theological Foundation: see p.219

Alligator Removal Services

"Nothing will ever separate us! You are my best friend in the whole wide world." That's what Alice said to Edie.

"No, nothing will separate us because we are the best friends ever," replied Edie. They did everything together; they played at school together, they studied together. They stayed over at each other's houses and talked late into the night under the blankets using flashlights. Wherever you saw Alice, you saw Edie and if you saw Edie, you saw Alice. They were always together!

On the day that the leads for the school musical were announced, the girls were walking back home through the park. Edie was really excited because she had been given the female lead to the musical.

"I can't believe it! Really, Alice, I can't believe it. My mother says I have a beautiful voice, but that's the first time I've ever tried to get a part in a musical. I would have been happy getting a small part like you but then I hit all those high notes without squeaking. I thought we'd just be singing in the chorus together. I can hardly wait to tell my family. Come on, let's run home!"

Even though Alice knew she had not done well at the tryouts and felt lucky even to be in the chorus, she felt like she'd just been hit. She couldn't breathe. Her stomach hurt and she felt like she was going to be sick. She turned her back on Edie and instead of running with Edie toward their neighborhood, she ran in the opposite direction across the park. Alice ran and ran until she found herself by the edge of the brook that bordered the park. Tears ran down her cheeks, sobs kept escaping out of her closed lips. Nothing like this had ever happened before.

"Edie is the worst friend in the whole wide world. 'A small part like you ... squeaking on the high notes' Arghhh! I hate her. I'm never going to talk to her again!"

That was the beginning of the 'great silence' between the two girls. Alice refused to take any phone calls from Edie. She refused to sit by her on the bus and she refused to talk with her at school. If Edie tried to join a group of girls where Alice was talking, Alice would find a reason to leave quickly without even looking at her.

Uncle Sol kept track of the children in the neighborhood, so it wasn't long before he was aware that something was very wrong between the two girls who had been best of friends. One afternoon when Edie was getting ready to leave Uncle Sol's yard, the older neighbor moved to open the garden gate for her. As she smiled and started to pass through, he asked, "Where's Alice these days, Edie? I'm not used to seeing the two of you apart." Edie's smile instantly drained away, "Uncle Sol, she's not speaking to me. I don't know if you heard I got the lead in the school musical, but I said something really dumb to her the day the parts were assigned. I know I hurt her feelings, but I've tried and tried to say, 'I'm sorry' but she just won't let me. I don't know what else to do. I miss her so much and I don't think she misses me at all. It's like she hates me, all because of this dumb musical. I wish I'd never gotten the part."

"Oh, now Edie," Uncle Sol said patting her shoulder, "it's a great privilege to be a lead and you have the talent to do it. I don't think you meant to hurt Alice's feelings, did you?"

"You know I didn't, Uncle Sol. It was one of those stupid things that slips out of your mouth before you even think about what it will do. I just wish she'd let me talk to her," Edie sighed.

"I'm sure there's a way for the two of you to patch things up between you," Uncle Sol reassured her. Edie could only hope he was right as she walked home.

Not long after that, Uncle Sol answered a knock at his door. He smiled as he opened the screen door for Alice who happened to be holding a plate full of cookies. "Well, hello, Alice. What's the occasion for cookies?" he asked.

"Mom and I were making cookies for the bake sale at school tomorrow and we thought you'd like to have some for all your extra backyard visitors," Alice answered.

"That's great! Thank you to both of you," Uncle Sol took the plate from Alice and placed it on the kitchen counter. "I do seem to go through cookies awfully fast around here. And fortunately, I don't get to eat too many of them myself." Uncle Sol laughed as he patted his stomach.

"Uh, Uncle Sol, since nobody else is around, could I talk with you for a minute?"

"Why sure, Alice. What's on your mind," the older neighbor asked, fully anticipating her answer.

"Well, I have a problem," Alice paused and took a deep breath, "a really huge problem."

Uncle Sol just waited for Alice to speak when she was ready.

"You know how Edie and I have been friends forever? I don't know if you've noticed that we haven't been hanging out together at all lately."

"I have noticed."

"It all started with the school musical try-outs. All of us girls wanted the lead. I mean, who wouldn't? But Edie and I both thought that neither one of us had a chance and that we'd be happy singing in the chorus together. Well, I did really badly at the try-outs; I was so nervous my voice cracked on the high notes. It was awful. I just wanted the song to get over with so I could escape. And Edie did great. She was sooo good and I was so happy for her. I think it was the best she'd ever sung. And that wasn't so bad. But then Edie got the lead and she made this comment about me "squeaking" during try-outs and it really hurt. And every time I see her I just remember what she said. I mean, if she were my best friend, why would she say something to hurt me like that? I just can't believe how rotten that was, especially since she got the lead and everyone's making such a fuss over her. I can't stand to even see her. Everybody keeps asking what's happened, why we aren't around each other. Edie keeps trying to talk to me, right in front of everyone. I hate her, Uncle Sol, I just hate her!" Alice stared at the kitchen floor, but tears were gathering around the corners of her eyes.

"Oh, Alice, it's really painful when a friend hurts us, whether they did it on purpose or not."

"Oh, I think she did it on purpose," Alice quickly responded.

"You can't be so sure about things like that unless you talk to her. Umm, let me pour you a little milk to go with a cookie or two," Uncle Sol said as he walked over to the refrigerator. "I've got a story I think you might find useful."

Uncle Sol returned from a back room in his house with a small picture book in his hand. As Alice munched the cookies, Uncle Sol began:

> Once there were two very good friends. They'd been friends practically from birth. In fact, neither one of them could ever remember not being friends. They did everything together. Angie and Tara were inseparable. Well, it so happened that one day Tara said something that really hurt her friend's feelings and Angie decided never to be friends again.
>
> Now, as Angie was walking back home alongside the brook that ran nearby the school, she saw a strange looking rock. At least she thought it was a rock. "I'm going to take this rock and carry it as a reminder of how awful my 'best' friend was to me today. Every time I touch this rock in my pocket I'll remember I don't ever want to be friends with her again!" she said to herself as she stuffed it in her pocket.
>
> Angie went home and for the first time ever, the girls didn't call each other that night and they didn't talk to each other all the next day or the next. They no longer sat at the same table at lunch and they didn't meet each other at recess. All this time, the rock in Angie's pocket

was acting very strangely. At first Angie couldn't be sure, but it felt like the rock began to wiggle right in the middle of a math lesson. By the time school was out, she was sure the "rock" was moving. It was alive, Angie was sure of that.

"Oh, I wonder what it could be? Maybe it's a duckling! No, the shell would have broken in my pocket. Maybe it's a platypus like we read about in geography. They live near water, but … I don't live in Australia."

When she got home, she closed the door to her bedroom before she cautiously removed the "rock" from her pocket. Looking at it very closely, Angie could see "the rock" wiggling and moving as something was trying to break out. She wanted to help the little creature, whatever it was, to hatch, but she remembered her grandfather had once said that the hard work of hatching helped baby birds gain their strength. So she carefully put the egg in a box on her desk.

The next day at school, Tara tried again to talk with Angie, but Angie just turned away. That afternoon, Angie rushed home after school to check the egg. It was hatching. Angie carefully picked up the egg and watched in amazement as a perfect baby alligator began to crawl out of its shell while looking right at her. Baby alligators are not very cute, but it belonged to Angie. It was hers alone. She began to carry the baby alligator everywhere.

Alice moved around to Uncle Sol's side of the table and sat next to him so she could see the funny illustrations in the homemade book. It was obvious to Alice that some child had drawn them.

Tara realized she had hurt Angie's feelings when she said that Angie shouldn't enter the art contest, but she hadn't meant to. What she really meant was that she didn't want Angie to be disappointed and it came out all wrong and she wanted Angie to know that. But every time Tara even tried to speak to Angie, to ask her to forgive her, Angie just turned away. That is when the strangest thing began to happen. Every time Tara asked Angie to forgive her and Angie refused, the baby alligator grew. Each time Angie relived that awful moment after art class when Tara had hurt her feelings, the alligator grew some more.

At first, she rather liked being the owner of an alligator. And in the beginning Angie didn't really notice that it was getting bigger. But soon the alligator was too big to put in her pocket so she had to carry it in her backpack. She began to feel the weight of the alligator for it had gotten to be quite large and very, very heavy. Angie finally decided she couldn't carry the alligator in her backpack anymore. But that didn't stop the alligator. It simply would not leave her alone. It followed her everywhere she went.

Alice stopped Uncle Sol from turning the page as she studied the drawing of the oversized alligator following the girl to school. She smiled as she shook her head, taking her hand away so he could go on.

> The bigger the alligator got, the more the other children avoided her. Everyone was afraid of Angie and her alligator. At school, in her neighborhood, everywhere in town the children talked about Angie.
> "That alligator is always with her!"
> "Did you see its teeth? I'm afraid it's going to bite me!"
> "Have you seen it move? I think it could catch me even if I ran!"
> Angie was so lonely. Nobody wanted to be her friend except Tara, but Angie still turned away from her old best friend. And each time she did, the alligator continued to grow larger.
> Finally, Angie was so miserable that she walked next door to Grandfather's house and standing at his front

door, she blurted out, "How do I get rid of this dumb alligator? I don't want it any more. Nobody wants to be my friend. It's ruining my life!"

"Why don't you tell me how you got the alligator in the first place?" said Grandfather.

"I found this rock. Well, I thought it was a rock and I put it in my pocket and then it started to hatch and this alligator came out. It was little to start with, but now it is so big and I just want to get rid of it." Grandfather suspected there was more to the story that Angie just didn't want to tell. He recognized this kind of alligator and knew it couldn't grow unless it was fed regularly with strongly held memories of hurtful things said or done to the owner.

"Hmmm … there is only one thing to do, Angie. You have to stop feeding it and really let it go," replied Grandfather.

"But I've tried to let it go, Grandfather. I put it down so I wouldn't have to carry it anymore. No matter how fast I run and even if I hide, it still follows me everywhere." Angie began to cry. "I just want friends again. I hate this alligator. You've got to help me!"

"Here's my suggestion, Angie," Grandfather said. "You need to go back to where you picked it up and REALLY let it go. You must not feed it again, not once. Only then will the alligator leave you for good."

Angie sighed, "Okay, Grandfather. I'll try again."

At first Angie was so upset she couldn't even recall the exact spot where she had picked up the alligator. As she looked into its cold yellow eyes and moved her gaze to its sharp teeth, its rough skin and long tail, she suddenly remembered.

"Hey, I didn't pick YOU up. I picked up a rock. At least I thought it was a rock, just to remind me of how mean Tara was and how much she hurt my feelings. I guess that means I have to take you back to the brook."

Now that was the tricky part—getting the alligator to go back to the brook. Angie started to walk to the park, but the alligator suddenly refused to follow her. She put a leash on the alligator and she began to tug and pull to get that alligator to move in the direction of the park. It wouldn't budge and Angie wasn't strong enough to force it to move.

"I just want you to disappear!" she wailed at the alligator. She got behind it and tried to push the alligator toward the brook, but it dug all four feet into the ground. Angie couldn't budge the beast a single inch. For all her effort, Angie and the alligator were still on the sidewalk just outside her house, not one bit closer to the brook. Angie just sat down beside the creature and began to cry.

"I'll help you, Angie," said a voice softly. Angie looked up. To her surprise, there was Tara. Even though Angie had ignored Tara for weeks, even though she had turned away from every effort Tara had made to start up a conversation, she was desperate to get rid of the alligator.

"All right, Tara," Angie said as she got up and wiped her tears on the back of her hand. "I'm trying to get this alligator back to the brook in the park."

The two girls tugged and pulled the alligator all the way to the brook. At the brook's edge, Angie slipped the leash off the alligator, but it didn't just disappear like Angie thought it would.

"Oh, no! Grandfather said you would disappear if I got you back to the brook! What's wrong? Disappear! Disappear, Alligator! Disappear!" Angie was so upset she almost didn't hear Tara saying,

"I'm really sorry about what I said, Angie. I really want to be friends. I've missed you so much … please forgive me…"

All of a sudden Angie stopped crying, "What did you say?"

"I said I'm really sorry about what I said, Angie. I want to be best friends again. I've missed you so much, please forgive me."

Angie looked at her old best friend. She reached out for Tara's hand and said, "Oh Tara, I've missed you, too. I do forgive you. Will you forgive me?"

"Oh yes, Angie … yes!" And with that, the alligator disappeared just like Grandfather had said it would.

Alice and Uncle Sol just sat there for a minute. The only sound was the hum of the refrigerator. "Where'd that book come from, Uncle Sol?" Alice asked, finally breaking the silence.

"Well, it's actually a story I wrote for my daughter when she was having a bit of trouble with a very good friend. Sort of like you and Edie. She drew pictures for it and we made it our 'home-made' book."

"Hmmm … did she and her friend fix things up?" Alice asked.

Uncle Sol had been looking through the pictures again, but he stopped and looked at Alice. "As a matter of fact, they did. They are still friends to this day."

"You know the other kids have been telling me that Edie didn't mean to hurt my feelings and she wants to be friends again."

"I've heard that, too," Uncle Sol added. Alice sat quietly thinking for a moment.

"I think I've got an alligator, Uncle Sol," Alice confided.

"I think there's a way to get rid of it, Alice."

"Yeah, I think there is, too," Alice answered back. And as the young neighbor slid off the kitchen stool, she looked at her older neighbor across the counter,

"Well, I'm pretty tired of the alligator that's following me around," she announced.

"I never liked the alligators that followed me, either. That's why I learned the secret of how to get rid of them."

"Okay, here I go, Uncle Sol. I am going to get rid of an alligator. Wish me luck!" Alice headed out the door and down the steps. When she got to the gate she didn't head for home. She turned toward Edie's house and started to run.

Matthew 18:15-35

Theological Foundation: see p.220
Guide for Non-religious Settings: see p.250

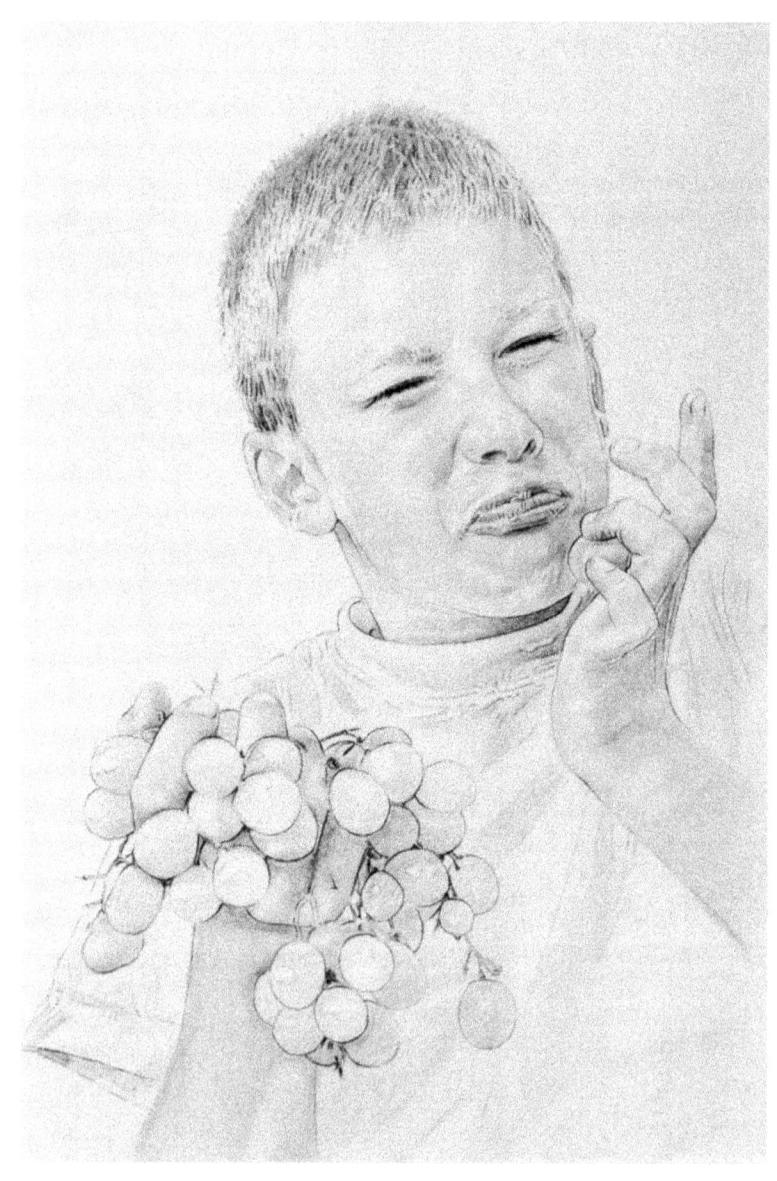

No Rushing Allowed

"Those grapes look ripe to me, Uncle Sol," Will said as he watched his retired neighbor clip a single grape from a bunch here and a single grape there. It was finally fall in the neighborhood. Will and the other children had watched the grapes grow all summer from little, tiny nubs to the big bunches they were now. "Uncle Sol, I have an idea ... why don't you just give me the grapes you're cutting off so I can eat them?" Will loved grapes; they were better than candy to him and he really wanted to eat all these grapes Uncle Sol was clipping off the bunches and throwing on the ground.

Uncle Sol chuckled, "Oh Will, you wouldn't like these. They aren't ready yet."

"But they're purple, Uncle Sol. They look like they'd taste great!"

"I know they *look* ready, but they're not really very sweet yet. In fact, I'm "thinning" the bunches just a little so the grapes can get even bigger in the next couple of weeks without splitting the skins."

"Well, it still seems like a waste to me," grumped Will. He didn't really understand Uncle Sol's idea of 'thinning', so he just kept watching.

Uncle Sol looked at his watch. "Oops, I've got to stop and do the rest later. I've got an appointment I can't miss, Will. You can come back later if you want. It'll be a couple of hours, but then I'll be here the rest of the afternoon."

Will watched Uncle Sol back out of his garage and drive away for his appointment. "This is perfect timing," Will thought to himself, "I can help Uncle Sol finish thinning his grapes and do it my way." He glanced around the neighborhood and once he was sure no other kids were in sight, he walked back into Uncle Sol's garden and made his way over to the grape arbor. Luckily there was a bench attached right onto the sides of the arbor. Climbing up on the bench, he put his plan into action.

"Uncle Sol didn't touch this bunch, so I'll thin it for him." Will took a big purple grape in his fingers and pulled it off the bunch. "Instead of wasting the grapes like Uncle Sol, I'll just eat them. Then there's no mess on the ground either." Will popped the grape into his mouth.

"Ughhh, that's not a very sweet one." Will's wrinkled nose and squinted eyes exclaimed how sour the grape really was.

"Maybe that was just a bad one," Will thought as he reached for another grape that looked like it would taste better. He popped that grape into his mouth, too. "That's better, but it's still not as sweet as last year's."

Will searched for riper looking grapes and then he "thinned" them, carefully putting them in his mouth instead of wasting them. While the taste wasn't very good, he was getting used to the sour bite of each grape as he first squeezed it between his teeth. He kept hoping he'd find sweeter ones. Unfortunately, he hadn't really been paying attention to what Uncle Sol had been doing. Uncle Sol had taken off just a few grapes here and there from each bunch, but Will kept sampling grapes off the same bunch until there were only really greenish looking ones left. Then moving on to other bunches of grapes, he continued his search for the sweet purple ones he remembered from previous years.

"They're all awful," Will thought to himself as he finally jumped down off the bench. "Uncle Sol's grapes aren't any good this year at all!" He looked over the bunches of grapes he had 'thinned' and they didn't look anything like the ones Uncle Sol had already finished. In fact, Will's bunches looked limp and nearly empty with barely a hint of purple color while Uncle Sol's bunches looked much fuller with lots of purple color mixed with the green. He wasn't sure that Uncle Sol would be happy with the job he'd done, so he slipped out of Uncle Sol's backyard into the field and then over to his own house without anyone ever seeing him. And just for good measure, he decided to stay clear of Uncle Sol's backyard for awhile.

Will loved the fall weather. Every morning when he joined the other children at the bus stop, there was frost on the grass, but each afternoon when he got home it was warm and sunny. The weather was perfect for playing outside. What he didn't know was that it was also perfect for ripening grapes.

Finally, the day came that all the children in the neighborhood had come to expect in the fall. Uncle Sol greeted the children right at the bus stop. "Today's harvest day if anyone's interested." Cheers erupted from the kids pouring off the bus. "After you've changed your clothes all of you are invited to help me harvest the grapes."

The grape harvesters were laughing and talking as they made their way into Uncle Sol's backyard and over to the grape arbor. "Now, I've got a bag for each of you so you can take your grapes home to share. Who's going to be first?" Hands shot up everywhere. "Okay, Helen, you're the youngest. Let's have you go first." Uncle Sol lifted the little girl up so she could cut her own grapes. The other kids could all manage to reach bunches by standing on the benches.

"Is that everyone?" He asked, checking to see if every child's bag was full. Will was standing there along with everyone else, but he hadn't even picked up a bag from the pile. "Will, it's your turn," Uncle Sol said.

"No thanks, Uncle Sol, I don't want to take any grapes home."

"That's quite a change for you, Will. I thought you loved grapes."

"Uhhh, I used to Uncle Sol, but I don't anymore."

Uncle Sol nodded, "Okay." But he immediately guessed what had happened to Will's love of grapes. When he'd gotten home from his appointment the day that Will had decided to 'help' thin the grapes, Uncle Sol had gone back to the arbor to rake up the grapes he'd thrown on the ground and to finish thinning the rest of the bunches. That was when he had discovered a couple of bunches of grapes that were completely missing any purple grapes on them. And there were other bunches that were considerably smaller than Uncle Sol had remembered. When he had looked around, he had noticed kid-size dirty footprints on the bench of the arbor underneath the bunches that were so bare. That's when he had figured out that he'd gotten a little extra "help" from a certain young neighbor. But he had decided he'd wait for the right time to talk with Will.

When the harvesting was done and the other children got ready to leave with their full bags, Uncle Sol said, "Will, I need some help cleaning up; will you stay a few minutes?"

"Sure, Uncle Sol." Will started breathing a little faster. He could feel his pulse speeding up, too. He had a sinking feeling he'd been 'found out'. He helped Uncle Sol carry the tools back to the garage and then he helped clear the picnic table of the cookies and juice that were left over from the "Harvest Party". Inside Uncle Sol's kitchen, he was really sweating even though it wasn't very hot. "I'll just finish clearing the table and then I've got to get home, Uncle Sol." Will managed to keep his voice steady.

"Oh, that's fine, Will. Hey, I'm sorry you lost your love of grapes. Are you sure no one else in your family would like some? I have plenty." Before Will could grab the words and stuff them back in his mouth, he answered, "Uncle Sol, your grapes aren't very good this year. They're just not as sweet as they were last year and I really only like super sweet grapes."

"I know that's the way you like them, Will." Then he added, "You know, when you eat grapes before they're ripe, they just can't be as good as they will eventually be. Like they are right now, in fact."

Will realized right then that Uncle Sol knew he'd helped himself to more grapes back when Uncle Sol was "thinning" them. Will's head hung down … he just stared at the floor. "Uncle Sol, I just thought I'd help you thin the grapes, so I ate one and then I ate another and I hoped they would taste better, but they weren't very sweet and I guess I ate so many trying to find some sweet ones that I got sick when I got home. I didn't listen to you. I thought I could tell what a ripe grape looked like."

"Here, taste this one, Will." The boy looked up. Uncle Sol was holding out a plump, purple grape in his open hand. He hesitated and then slowly took it from Uncle Sol and popped it into his mouth. When he bit down on the grape, the sweet juice filled his mouth.

"Ummmm, that's the way I like them." Then Will looked right into Uncle Sol's eyes as he apologized, "I'm sorry I came back and thinned your grapes without permission, Uncle Sol. I was just sure you were completely wasting so many good grapes and ... well, of course, now I know you weren't. You were right ... again."

"Will, your apology is accepted. You know, grapes do take time to sweeten in the fall. They need warm days and frosty nights to get just the right sweetness. After lots of days like that it's finally time to harvest. I know it's pretty hard to be patient."

"It *really* is, Uncle Sol. Everything seems to take so long. My mother says I'm always trying to wish my life away because I'm wishing that school vacation would come, or that my birthday would hurry up ... or," he added with a sheepish smile, "that the grapes would get ripe quicker."

"You just can't rush the time, Will. There is an order to the seasons. Fall moves into winter, winter moves into spring, spring moves into summer and then it begins again. You know, the same thing is true for our lives. There is an order to it all and patience helps us wait and enjoy the part of life we're in before life moves us on into another part."

"Sometimes I wish I were a grown-up. Then maybe I'd already know how to be patient."

"Don't count on it, Will," Uncle Sol chuckled. "Not all grown-ups know how to be patient and you don't have to be a grown-up to start practicing. Try this: think of yourself as a branch on my grapevine. What happened to you last spring, that is, to the branches of the vine on the arbor?"

"Okay, uh, let's see," Will smiled as he began to imagine. "First I sprouted leaves and those funny little flowers that had all those little teeny, tiny grapes on them."

"Right, then what?"

"Uh … then I just grew. The branches got longer and the leaves got bigger. No, I mean *I* got longer and my leaves got bigger." Breaking off the imagining, Will continued, "I remember how it seemed like nothing was happening to the grapes for the longest time. They just hung there, but I guess the leaves were still growing even then."

"That's true, and something was happening even when it didn't look like it, right?"

"Yeah, because when we came back from vacation, it seemed like the grapes were suddenly huge green balls, and they hadn't been when we left."

"And then they started to turn color and finally they were ripe, a good while *after* they turned the right color," said Uncle Sol as he winked at Will.

"Yeah, just because something *looks* ripe, doesn't mean it *is*." Will's serious look gave way to a bit of a smile.

"So what's the life lesson to be learned here, Philosopher?" Uncle Sol asked. ("Philosopher" was the nickname that Uncle Sol had given Will because the young neighbor was always trying to figure out the deeper meaning of ordinary events around the neighborhood.)

Will straightened up trying to look the part of the neighborhood philosopher and replied in an official voice, "That you can't rush time … that I'm like a branch on your grapevine and I am growing even when it doesn't look like it. And I can trust that there is a right time for everything … and that I can be patient because it will all work out."

"That's a very good start, Will. Remember that; it'll help."

"That's going to be a hard one, Uncle Sol. I'm still a kid."

"I'll tell you a secret, Will; it's still a hard one for adults."

"Thanks for the encouragement." Will gave Uncle Sol one of his impish grins as he followed Uncle Sol out to the grape arbor to pick some bunches to take home.

Jeremiah 29:4-11

Theological Foundation: see p.223
Guide for Non-religious Settings: see p.252

Neighborhood MVP

All babies are beautiful. Human babies, animal babies even baby plants or trees can be beautiful to people who love them. Uncle Sol loved plants and trees almost as much as he loved people; and he loved people a lot. All summer Uncle Sol took very special care of the two baby apple trees. Tall and slender with small tufts of leaves at the ends of their spindly branches, they almost looked like lean, trim cheerleaders with pompoms raised over their heads.

"Now I want all of you to be careful around my two new babies," Uncle Sol told all the neighborhood kids gathered in his yard the day he planted them. "These are no ordinary apple trees. Their great, great, great, grandma apple tree was the kind that farmers during the American Revolution used to make cider. I'm hoping to get them to grow. Then, someday, if we're lucky, we can make our own cider," Uncle Sol patted the little tree branches and smiled like a proud daddy. The children laughed and promised they'd be careful.

After their leaves dropped off in the fall, the baby trees looked pretty pitiful. The kids continued to be careful around them, but it was hard to remember they were there in the lawn. Sometimes, as the sun started to go down, the little tree trunks nearly disappeared because they blended into the naked branches of the hedge around Uncle Sol's backyard … especially if you were in a hurry and not paying attention … which is exactly what happened to Rocky. He was playing laser tag with his friend Nick. They always liked to play just as the sun was going down because the shadows made it easier to hide and then sneak up on each other. Uncle Sol's yard was the best place in the whole neighborhood because he had so many bushes and trees and especially because he always welcomed the kids.

Nick had just come around the corner of Uncle Sol's house and spotted Rocky, but Rocky had seen him out of the corner of his eye. The teen turned to run as fast as he could. Zigzagging across the yard, Rocky forgot about everything except dodging Nick's laser. It was just the right—or maybe the wrong—time of day and Rocky simply didn't see the thin trees as he burst across the yard. One moment he was running and in the next moment he felt himself ricocheting from one tree trunk to another.

When Rocky opened his eyes after crashing to the ground he realized instantly what had happened. He jumped up and to his horror, there were both of Uncle Sol's trees flattened on the lawn. He quickly reached down to try to stand the thin little trunk of one of the trees upright. When he let go of it, it flopped pathetically back down on the lawn. It was no use; Rocky's body weight had snapped the trunk off right at the ground.

By this time, Nick was at Rocky's side. "Oh man, are you in trouble. You know Uncle Sol asked us to be careful around his new trees. C…c…can they stand?" Nick reached down, trying to get the other tree to stand up when he, too, realized both trunks had been snapped off right where the trunk emerged from the dirt. "Oh, this is bad … really bad."

"I know, I know," Rocky replied as a sick feeling swept over him. Uncle Sol had really been a special friend to Rocky ever since he had moved into the neighborhood. The truth is, Rocky had been a very angry young teen when he had first arrived and he'd done some real damage to Uncle Sol's gardens on purpose. Uncle Sol's forgiveness and unwillingness to give up on the boy had turned Rocky's life around. He loved Uncle Sol as if he were his own grandfather and there was nothing Rocky wouldn't do for him. Now this—he had single-handedly destroyed Uncle Sol's carefully tended trees in the blink of an eye.

"Hey, Rocky, look at your jacket." Rocky looked down at the sleeve. There was a ragged rip from the elbow to the cuff. It was ruined.

"Great. Just great. I've got a game tomorrow and I'm supposed to wear this when we travel. Now I'll have Coach mad at me along with Uncle Sol."

"Well, you've really done it this time, Rocky. Hey, I'm really sorry. I *am* ... but I've gotta go. I told my mom I'd be home before supper to help." With that, Nick took off, leaving Rocky alone in the yard with the broken trees, torn jacket and shadows fast blocking out the remaining dusky light.

Just then, headlights swept across the lawn and stopped on the garage door. The familiar sound of the garage door opener slowly winding the door up and out of sight told Rocky that Uncle Sol was home. "This is it. I gotta tell him," the boy said to himself as he started walking over to the side of the garage. "Need any help with the groceries, Uncle Sol?"

"Why sure, Rocky. Here. Have a good game of laser tag?"

"Huh? Laser tag? Oh yeah, it was good until the end."

Uncle Sol heard the tone in Rocky's voice, "And so what happened at the end?"

"I don't know really, but I'm sorry, Uncle Sol ... really sorry."

"Sorry about what?" A note of concern crept into Uncle Sol's response.

"I didn't mean to do it. I just wasn't paying attention or something. I really don't know how I managed to wreck them both."

Uncle Sol put the grocery bags down on the driveway. "Why don't you show me what you're talking about, Rocky?" Rocky led Uncle Sol over to the flattened trees. Even in the near darkness Uncle Sol could see that where there had been two spindly tree trunks there was nothing. Rocky pointed to the ground. "I think I just snapped them both off at the ground, but I'm not sure how I did it. I was running one minute and then the next minute I was on the ground and they were both destroyed. I'm so sorry. Is there anything I can do to save them ... graft them back into place or something?"

"Well," said the old neighbor straightening up after bending down to inspect the damage, "there really is nothing you can do. It's too late in the season to even think of grafting and I don't think it would be possible anyway. Next spring I'll have to start again."

Rocky's shoulders slumped. He already knew what Uncle Sol said was true, but to hear the sadness in Uncle Sol's voice and the finality of it all just made Rocky feel horrible. "Let me get the groceries for you, Uncle Sol," Rocky said as they turned toward the driveway.

The darkness accentuated the silence between the two as they carried the bags from the driveway into the kitchen. "Maybe I could pay for the new trees, Uncle Sol. I earn money taking care of some of my neighbors' pets when they go on vacation, and I rake lawns. I know I could earn enough to pay for them by next spring." Rocky scrambled to find a way to repair the damage. "No, Rocky, thank you for offering, but it was an accident. Just help me get the new ones started next season, okay?"

Rocky started for the door when Uncle Sol stopped him, "Hey, let me look at that jacket." The old man ran his fingers over the ragged tear on the teen's team jacket and shook his head. "That can't be fixed in any way that will hide the rip. I know Coach doesn't want any player on the team looking patched together for a game."

"Well, I don't know what I'm gonna do. I've got to be on the bus at 7:00 tomorrow morning. Coach is gonna be really mad." As Rocky reached for the doorknob he stopped and said, "Uncle Sol, ... h, h, how do you know Coach?"

"My son, Hank, played for him, too, Rocky. Coach isn't exactly a young man, you know."

"Yeah, we call him 'old man' behind his back," Rocky said with a smile, "but he's still a good coach ... just kinda demanding. Guess ya *gotta* be to have so many winning teams.

Anyway, I can count on getting yelled at about this jacket no matter what I do to try and fix it."

"Hold on a minute, Rocky. I think my son's team jacket is still here."

"Oh, that's okay, Uncle Sol. Really, I'm sure it wouldn't go with the uniforms we wear now. And besides, it's your son's jacket. I wouldn't want to risk wrecking it."

Uncle Sol disappeared into a bedroom and came out with the jacket under his arm. "I think you'll be surprised, Rocky. The color is perfect … and the style has hardly changed. And I think Coach will smile when he sees this."

"Uh, Uncle Sol, I don't know. Really, I'll just take what's coming to me. I deserve it for being so stupid."

"Put it on, Rocky." Uncle Sol held the jacket open and shook it like a matador in front of the teen. Rocky, took a deep breath, sighed, peeled off his own jacket and slipped his arms into the waiting sleeves. It fit perfectly.

The boy moved cautiously over to the mirror in the hallway. "I guess the school hasn't changed the jackets that much, has it? I mean this practically looks like mine." Only then did he notice the embroidered award on the left front panel: MVP 1997.

"Oh, Uncle Sol, I can't wear this. I'm no MVP. I'm a good player, but I can't. Really, I can't."

"Rocky, it will be okay. I know Coach. He wouldn't like that ripped up sleeve, but I'm pretty sure he'd be okay with this … at least for tomorrow. You wear it. Besides, I like the look of that on you."

"I don't know, Uncle Sol. It's pretty strange to think about wearing your son's jacket. It's like I'm pretending to be something I'm not." Rocky shook his head and softly said, almost in a whisper, "MVP. He must have been a great player. The only way I'll get this award is in my dreams."

"What do you mean? You *are* the MVP right now. I'm looking at you." Uncle Sol's eyes twinkled.

"But Uncle Sol, it's your son's jacket. I didn't earn it."

"When I look at you wearing that jacket, I see my son Hank. I see his determination, his skill, his leadership, his humility ... that's what I see."

"Then you need your glasses fixed, Uncle Sol 'cause I'm none of those things." Rocky pulled at the sleeve to remove the jacket.

"Just got the glasses, they work fine." The old neighbor walked over to the kitchen stool and sat down, "Listen, Rocky, you see all the things you aren't. I see what you are and what you're becoming." Then more quietly, the old neighbor added, "Leave the jacket on, Son."

"Uncle Sol, listen to me. I'm not like your son at all. From what I've heard around the neighborhood, Hank was just a great guy to be around all the time. He was so nice to everyone, especially all the little kids who are now teenagers like me. It sounds like he was an awful lot like *you* ... just plain good ... all the time. That's not me. I've never been good. I mean I'm trying now, but Uncle Sol, I've wrecked your garden more than once. I've ignored your advice so many times and I've gotten into so much trouble." Uncle Sol smiled and shook his head as he looked at the very earnest teenager standing in front of him. "You know what I'm talking about, Uncle Sol. I'd like to be like Hank. No, actually I wish I could *be* Hank. I wish I could be part of your family, I wish I could be like you." The ticks of the clock on the kitchen wall could be counted as Rocky stared at the floor.

"Rocky, it's my turn. I want you to listen to what I'm saying. In that jacket, I do see you ... *and* I see Hank. I know what you've done. I know what you've ignored. But the minute I invited you into my garden, I considered you one of my neighbors. I welcomed you like I would my own son because that's how I see you. That's how I see all the children and teens here—as if they are my own. No matter what any of you do, you really can't lose that identity I've given you."

Rocky looked up at his neighbor, one of those long searching looks trying to see if Uncle Sol was really being honest, really sincere about saying how he thought of each kid in the neighborhood as his own. But Uncle Sol just looked back with that smile in his eyes that told Rocky the old neighbor actually meant every word. Slowly, it dawned on Rocky that he really *was* the MVP in Uncle Sol's eyes. He knew in the very core of himself that even if he messed up again he could not lose the special place he had in Uncle Sol's heart. For the first time, he knew beyond a doubt he was completely welcome in Uncle Sol's life just because that was the way Uncle Sol was.

Breaking the silence Rocky stammered, "I ... I ... I guess I've kinda wondered about the reason why you treat everyone the way you do. I mean, nobody else does that. People are nice ... mostly ... but you ... you're different. All of us know that. And as for me, well, you always let me come back. No matter how awful I've been. No matter what I've done. I wanna make you proud, Uncle Sol. I wanna be an MVP like Hank." Suddenly an impish grin crossed Rocky's face. "Mostly, I wanna quit messin' up your garden.!"

Uncle Sol put his hands on Rocky's shoulders, "Just get out there and play your best tomorrow. Coach will see the MVP I know and love." The shadows had disappeared into black silhouettes by the time Rocky stepped off the porch at Uncle Sol's. Funny how the path to his house seemed as bright as day for Uncle Sol's MVP as he jogged home. He knew he was going to have a great game in the morning.

Luke 3: 21-22
Mark 1: 9-11
Matthew 3:13-17

Theological Foundation: see p.225
Guide for Non-religious Settings: see p.254

Some Birthday!

Nick's eyes fluttered open. At last, it was finally here, the most special day of his year ... his birthday. He jumped out of bed, dressed as quickly as he could and raced eagerly downstairs.

Nick fully expected to see balloons and signs and gifts and cards all around the dining room table. That is the way it had been for as long as he could remember. But when he got downstairs and turned the corner, there was the dining room looking the same as ever. Just a table and chairs and the same bouquet of artificial flowers.

"Good morning, Nick," his mother called from the kitchen.

"Good morning, Mom. Hey, isn't it my birthday today?"

She sounded flustered. "Oh, good heavens ... what's the date today? Oh, good heavens, I guess it *is* your birthday. How could I have forgotten? Oh, Nick, I'm so sorry. Things have been so busy. Between being in charge of the fundraiser at your school, your brother's band's first performance and your dad's business trip, I've been completely preoccupied. I can't believe the day has just popped up." Nick's mom had come out of the kitchen and hugged her now officially teenaged son close to her. "We'll make it up to you this weekend, I promise. Now, don't you worry. Recognizing a birthday still counts even if it is not on the day," she said as Nick plunked down at the kitchen table to eat breakfast.

Nick was feeling pretty bad as he climbed on the bus to go to school. His own mother had forgotten his birthday and with his dad out of town there was no use hoping that this was just a bad joke. As he was riding along and feeling sorry for himself, an idea began to form in his mind. He didn't have to wait for other people to recognize his big day ... he could do it himself. He could create his own birthday party. The more he thought about it, the more he liked the idea and by the time he got to school, Nick had decided to do something about it. The moment Nick stepped into the hallway, he began to ask his friends who lived right in the neighborhood.

"Hey, Jon, today's my birthday. You want to come to a party at my house after school?"

"Oh, I'd like to Nick, but ... uh ... I can't. I have, uh ... I gotta do something else"

That was strange. Jon never had something else to do right after school because he always went home with Will and stayed there until his parents got home from work.

"Hey, Will, today's my birthday, and my mom forgot, but I'm gonna have a party at my house right after school anyway; can you come?"

"Uh, sorry Nick ... I'm going somewhere after school; maybe another day?" Will hurried down the hall to his class.

Nick had been feeling bad enough *before* getting turned down by his best friends, but now he was feeling even worse. During lunch, he asked other kids in the neighborhood if they could come to his party. Nobody could come. Each and every one had to go somewhere or do something after school.

"My mom forgets, my dad's away, my friends can't come. This is the worst birthday ever," Nick said to himself. He was feeling pretty sorry for himself when he got off the bus. His mother wasn't home when he arrived. He hadn't expected her, but the house seemed especially empty on his birthday. He wandered out into the backyard. He could hear the sounds of lawnmowers around the neighborhood, but he didn't hear the usual laughter and talking that often floated through the air to his yard. More often than not, neighborhood kids were playing in Uncle Sol's yard next door and because of that Nick never felt alone after school. This day, however, not a voice, not a sound came from his older neighbor's backyard. Nick looked at the ladder to his old tree house and decided to climb up. Once inside he set up an un-party for himself. As he finished singing "Happy Birthday to me, Happy Birthday to me, Happy Birthday poor Nick-with-no-friends ... Happy Birthday to me, " a voice came through the bushes,

"Did I hear that right? 'Poor Nick with no friends'?" It was Uncle Sol. With all the sounds of lawnmowers, Nick had not heard the muted scratching of the rake that his neighbor was using to smooth out the dirt around the new bushes he had planted near the tree house. "What's going on, Nick?"

Nick was so surprised and embarrassed to discover that anyone had heard him singing, he suddenly felt a bit shy. He took a deep breath and started to speak.

"Uncle Sol, my mother ... my own mother forgot my birthday. My dad is away on business, my brother is at soccer practice and all of my friends are busy. I tried to put together my own party and nobody could come. I've been deserted! What a crummy, awful birthday!" He went on at some length with a replay of nearly every minute since he had gotten out of bed.

Uncle Sol listened as Nick told his sad tale, but finally he said, "Nick, you know you really can't force a joyful surprise to happen and I've learned that you can't control the way people show their love for you. It's like this breeze in the garden this afternoon ... it comes and it goes. But on a warm day, it sure makes sense to turn your face toward it when it comes." Nick scrunched his nose and squinted his eyes like he always did when he tried to understand something a bit confusing ... and what Uncle Sol had said confused him. He couldn't see what breezes and turning your face to them had to do with a missed birthday.

Uncle Sol put a stop to Nick's effort to figure it out, "Hey, Nick, why don't you just come over and have some milk and cookies. I know its not a birthday cake, but if you use your imagination, it might work. And I'm sure we can find some of the kids in the neighborhood to join us." Nick looked doubt-ful, but he didn't want to disappoint Uncle Sol when he was obviously trying to make him feel better. He followed Uncle Sol up the stairs of his deck and just as the door opened, he heard "Surprise! Surprise! Nick, Happy Birthday!" And there they were, all his friends from the neighborhood who were "busy" after school and behind them was his mother, smiling with a beautiful birthday cake and right beside her was his dad and his brother.

Nick didn't know what to say. He didn't know what to do, but his heart was nearly ready to burst. He looked at Uncle Sol who was grinning from ear to ear and who leaned over and said, "I told you ... you can't control the way people show their love for you any more than you can control the breeze in the yard ... just enjoy it when it comes."

John 3:1-17

Theological Foundation: see p.228
Guide for Non-religious Settings: see p.256

The River Run

The river that feeds the lake near the neighborhood isn't huge by river standards ... only thirty to fifty feet across with lots of sand bars and grass. Giant-sized old trees and thick blackberry bushes line the steep banks making easy access difficult; but it is cool refreshment on hot summer afternoons. As children grow into teenagers, it is almost a rite of passage to start up at the old bridge about 10 miles from the lake and float down the river. Everyone looks forward to that day when parents finally relent and give permission to make the big trip.

One afternoon the older kids in the neighborhood had gathered on Uncle Sol's deck. They were regaling him with stories of their latest water adventure: a canoe trip on the lake where they had succeeded in swamping each other's canoes so often they never did get to their destination across the lake and back.

"You are just as wild in the water as my friends and I were," chuckled Uncle Sol. "Never could leave a guy dry in a canoe in the summer ... it just wasn't natural."

"Still isn't, Uncle Sol," laughed Rocky

"Well, I much preferred the lake to the river for just plain fun. The river needs your total attention, even when you're just floating," reflected Uncle Sol.

"Really? Why's that, Uncle Sol?" asked Edie.

Edie was more than a little interested. She had finally convinced her parents to let her float down the river and she wanted every bit of information she could get so that she might eliminate any surprises. She was an excellent swimmer and a take-charge kind of person, so no one was expecting the river trip to be very difficult for Edie.

"For one thing, the river is never the same two years in a row. The current is pretty fast and particularly in the places where it gets so narrow, it goes especially deep and has a way of pulling you where you don't necessarily want to go. And there are always the unexpected things like trees blown down at the water's edge falling into the river and making it nearly impossible to pass by the partly submerged branches," added the neighborhood's mentor.

"Gee, you make it sound sort of dangerous," Edie said reproachfully.

"Oh, it's not exactly dangerous, Edie, but you do have to pay attention all the time like Uncle Sol says." Nick was not about to be left out of the conversation since he'd had his first run just last year.

"It's just really important to stay with your tube. It's your life-preserver, especially if you get stuck in the branches. If something gets caught in the branches, the river tugs away at it, even if it means dragging it underwater instead of on top. You just don't want it to be you. That's why it's so important to stay on top with the tube," Uncle Sol spoke matter-of-factly. After a moment's hesitation he continued, "but there may be times though…" Uncle Sol stopped speaking and gazed over the teens' heads as if he were looking at something in the distance.

"There may be times though…" Edie prompted. She wanted to know the rest of the thought.

"Oh, there may be times … and you will never know when that might be … that the best advice is to not follow all the advice…"

"'The best advice is to not follow all the advice?' What does *that* mean?" Edie puzzled in her mind but before she could ask, David catapulted into the conversation.

"My first time was just two weeks ago and it was a piece of cake. There weren't any trees in the river, I mean there were no big ones. There are always a few branches on the sides, but they were easy to avoid. It wasn't a big deal and we had a blast! We each tied a small cooler to our tube so we had cold drinks on the way. It was awesome."

"My dad said he thinks I'm ready, so I'm trying to find some people to go with—"

David cut her off, jumping to his feet as he spoke: "Look no farther! I'm ready to be a river guide."

"Hey, *I* should be the river guide. I've done it three times so far," said Rocky. "If you want, Edie, I'll go with you."

"Well, you're not going to leave *me* out of this," said Nick. "When's this going to happen?"

"I guess as soon as I find out when my dad can take us up to the bridge," said Edie, her face flushed with a rush of mingled excitement and fear.

Three boys and a girl piled out of the truck the following blazing hot morning—a day perfect for river running. Edie's father helped lug the tubes down to the river's edge beneath the bridge. They had to duck as swallows swooped menacingly close to their heads while they scrambled down the dirt path. The birds never took kindly to intruders disrupting their nesting area underneath the bridge's deck beams.

"All right, boys, you watch after my little girl," said Edie's father as the girl glared at him.

"You should be telling me to watch out for *them*, Dad. They're the ones always needing help. Hey, don't forget to put the basket with all our shoes and towels on the picnic table at the park. We don't want to walk home barefoot and dripping wet!" shot back Edie, attempting to recover some dignity.

"Ah, you know I'm just teasing," her father said as he ruffled the hair on the top of her head. "Seriously now, be careful. Don't be so busy talking you miss what's going on around you. And remember, stay on your tube. Your mother is not wild about this anyway, so do me a favor and come back."

"Geez … another 'be-careful-talk.' Don't worry," piped up David, "I just did this a couple of weeks ago and everything was fine. Really."

"Okay, just the same, heads up," said Edie's father as he turned to walk up the path to the road.

The coolness of the river was a surprise as they waded out into the green-brown water. Edie felt the sand beneath her feet shiver and give way as the current tugged at her toes and her legs. A flutter of anticipation and apprehension swept over her as she slowly edged out past her knees.

"Okay, now just hop onto your tube and let the river do the rest," called out Rocky as he gracefully slid from standing beside the tube to sitting like a king on his throne. Immediately the current moved him away from the others. In quick succession, Nick, David and Edie were on their tubes, using their hands as paddles to catch up to Rocky.

"Hey, this is awesome," Nick called out.

"Yeah, it's cool," responded David.

"Like no where else," added Rocky.

Edie was speechless. For several minutes they just floated along, allowing the current to push them downriver at an amazingly swift pace.

"Hey, whaddayathink, Edie?" asked Rocky who had noticed that Edie, who always talked a lot, was absolutely silent.

"I'm, I'm … well … it's just so beautiful down here on the river … I mean these are places you just can't see from the road … not at all … the trees are so big when you see them from the water … and all the wild vines … I mean look at all the berries … blackberries, raspberries … and the birds … oh my gosh, my uncle would go crazy if he could see all the birds down here … and the way the sun twinkles through the leaves and makes patterns on the water … and the way the water ripples and bubbles up as it moves us … it *is* cool and awesome. I love it."

"Guess I should just leave you alone when you're quiet … I wasn't looking for an interview." The other boys laughed … and after hrrumphing at the teasing, Edie joined in.

"Okay, so I talk a lot … but you gotta admit, this is amazing."

The good natured bantering went on mile after mile.

It was David who noticed things were looking a bit different from just two weeks earlier. "Hey, look at those trees leaning into the river."

"Yeah, so?" said Nick.

"Well, they weren't like that two weeks ago. I wonder what happened."

"Well, it could've been that last thunderstorm we had. I heard on the news we had some insane wind gusts—like 70 miles an hour or something like that." Rocky always seemed to be up on the weather. Ever since he had nearly drowned in the lake because he hadn't paid attention to the spring thaw and its effect on ice, he'd become the neighborhood's resident weather observer. "Yeah, it probably was the thunderstorm. You know these trees don't have much to hold them to the bank so in a strong wind they can fall pretty easily."

The four friends threaded their way through the low overhanging branches by lying down as flat as they could on the tubes.

"That was crazy, trying not to get wiped off the tube," called out David over his back.

"I thought I was gonna get stuck there. I got a huge scratch from that one big branch," yelled Nick.

Edie didn't say anything. She had managed to lie flat enough, but the branches had scraped and pulled at her, like countless little hands grabbing to hold her back while the river had insistently pushed her tube forward. For a moment she had teetered on the brink of dunking. Her hair had caught in a passing branch and as she had reached to free it, the tube had nearly slipped out from underneath her.

"Hey, its okay, Edie, I'm sure that's the worst of it," yelled David after he had turned to float backwards and had seen the fright pass over his friend's face.

No sooner had David's words died away when, Rocky, Nick and Edie yelled,

"David, look out!"

David was oblivious to the impending obstacle in his path. The teens had just rounded another sharp bend and could see that a huge tree was completely spanning the river not far ahead. David wheeled his tube around just in time to smack into a small space between its branches.

The three others tried desperately to paddle against the current. All they did was succeed in slowing themselves down as they were pulled into the waiting branches. Within seconds all four teens were trapped by the tree and the river. The tree had fallen into the water just enough to make it impossible to pass under it … and it stuck out of the water so high that it looked more like a wall than a tree trunk from where the four sat, bouncing and bumping against the tree blockade.

'Oh, this is just great. What are we gonna do?" yelled Nick above the noise of water colliding with hundreds of branches bobbing and bouncing against the current.

"Can you see if it gets any better over by the bank?" called back Rocky. "I'm wondering if there's some room to go under it closer to the trunk or maybe at the tip. Then we could slip by it."

Edie used her legs to push away from the trunk. The force of the water rushing against the tube grabbed at the lowered edge and nearly flipped her. She frantically grabbed the tube and relaxed her legs allowing the water to shove her up against the trunk once again. A feeling of dread began to spread through Edie's entire body as she remembered warnings from her childhood before blurting out, "Oh my gosh … I almost went over … you know I've heard of kids who have been sucked under water near trees and then they get caught by branches and they can't get free because the current pins them. I don't want it to happen to us!"

"Neither do I, Edie. Now, come on you guys. We gotta think before we move." Rocky's voice betrayed his own rising fear.

"I just wanna get out of here," muttered David. Nick overheard him since they were pinned in the same spot. "but I don't know how we're gonna do it. Every time I move, the tube practically disappears under the surface. No way I can swim *under* this thing."

"Well you'd better not even try to get off your tube, that's insane. It's your life preserver!" yelled Rocky through the branches separating him from the two other boys.

"Can you grab that branch behind you, Nick?" Rocky was trying to peer through the leaves as he asked.

"I don't know, why?"

"I'm wondering if maybe we could pull ourselves over to the bank?" Rocky wasn't sure exactly how this would work, but it seemed like a possible way out.

"Okay, I'm gonna try."

Nick eased his hand out behind his head and felt the branch. In trying to turn his head just enough to look for a place to grab hold of the branch, the tube's side dipped too far underwater. Instantly, Nick was thrown off-balance and the tube flipped. He flailed at his slippery life preserver as it bounced up and down against the tree trunk, the current tugging at his legs, pulling them under the tree. He kicked with all his strength and managed to fight the current's tug just long enough to find David's outstretched hand. He started to grasp it when he realized that he'd only pull David into the water with him if he took his offer. At that moment of realization he managed to twist just enough to see another handhold to grab. His fingers found the branch he'd been reaching for in the first place and he grabbed on as tightly as he could. Terrified looks passed between Nick and David as Nick clung to the part of the branch that was above water. The force of the current kept dragging Nick's legs under the tree against the rough bark. The tube repeatedly hit him in the face as it bounced high against the tree wall. Nick was helplessly pinned.

"Nick, Nick!" screamed Edie. All she could see from where she was caught was the tube bouncing, riderless against the tree trunk.

"I'm ... o ... kay ... I'm ... st ... st ... uck" Nick's voice was shaky and his teeth were chattering. Cold water and fear were sapping both his strength and his courage.

"I say we just sit here until someone misses us," announced David. "Remember, we're not supposed to leave our tubes no matter what. And after what's happened to Nick, I'm not leaving mine. I'll sit here until we're rescued."

"Yeah, well that'll be hours and hours from now. And Nick's getting pretty cold. And how are they gonna find us anyway? Do you have any idea where we *are* on this river?" Rocky was exasperated with the suggestion, but he didn't have another solution either.

The teens bobbed in silence. The only sound was the rushing water as it slipped under branches and dived under the tree wall, leaving Edie, Nick, David and Rocky stranded. The four didn't hear the birds singing in the trees lining the bank, or the buzz of the heat bugs. They didn't feel the blistering heat. Summer had disappeared. There was only the river.

Edie was quiet. At first she had been too panicked to think. Bouncing and bumping against the tree trunk, she had been sure some unseen aqua hands would grab her and pull her beneath the surface to a watery grave. Then, when she had tried to push away from the tree wall and nearly flipped herself, she had become convinced that sitting still and waiting for help was the only solution, especially after Nick's mishap. But now she was simply quiet. She realized that just sitting still allowed her to feel relatively safe. Her mind was sifting through all the tales she'd ever heard of river trips from her older friends. Over and over the refrain repeated itself, "Don't leave your tube, it's your life-preserver."

Her eyes roamed over the tree trunk while a conversation went on back and forth in her head, "It really does look like a bridge. If we could just get up on it, then we probably could walk to the bank. Yeah, but look what happened every time the guys even leaned a little bit." "Remember stay on your tube," she could hear her father's last words to her before he had walked up the embankment to the car.

But there was another remembered voice repeating itself in her mind. At first it was so quiet she hardly noticed, but the words kept coming back more insistently with each bounce of the tube against the trunk, "Sometimes the best advice is to not follow all the advice." Suddenly, Edie was no longer puzzled about Uncle Sol's cryptic remark...

"The best advice is not to follow all the advice," Edie said it out loud to herself and a surge of energy and hope shot through her. "We've got to forget the tubes and climb out of here," yelled Edie.

"You're crazy," David hollered back, "I'm not moving until we get rescued!"

Undaunted Edie searched for a way to get up the trunk. Ever so slowly Edie drew her legs in toward her chest. The tube wobbled threateningly as it continued to bounce against the tree. She shifted her weight so that she was sitting more upright in the tube. As Edie focused on keeping her weight exactly in the middle of the tube she realized that it would not dip into the on-coming water and risk flipping. She had her eye on a branch that was sticking out like a flagpole on the side of a house. "If I can stand on the tube for just a second, I'd be able to jump and catch it and then pull myself up on the trunk..." Edie was talking to herself now as she worked up the courage to act.

Attempting to stand on tubes was part of the way all the kids played around in the lake where the water was calm. No one could actually stand on a tube for long without falling in, but it was always fun trying. Edie had mastered the ability to get to a standing position but this time 'a miss' meant 'a fall' into the current that would drag her under the tree to waiting branches beneath the surface where she could get trapped. She shuddered at the thought. Cautiously Edie began to turn on the tube so that she could be on her stomach. The grasping current of the river against her tube seemed to mock her, "I dare you to try!" Even that threat did not stop her. She managed to turn and recover as the tube lurched precariously into the current. "Okay..." Edie panted after passing the first hurtle. "I'm on my stomach ... now up on my hands and knees." The tube danced on the surface, bouncing against the trunk, but Edie's balance held. She pulled one foot onto the tube and then the other. "Edie, Now!" In a cat-like motion, Edie was up on her feet, letting go of the tube with her hands and leaping toward the outstretched branch, she caught it and used the wet bark for toeholds to scramble up onto the trunk.

"Edie!" yelled David… "How the heck…?"

But before David could even finish, Edie was bracing herself against a sturdy branch and reaching down to Nick.

"Th … th … th … anks … E … Edie…" was all Nick could manage as she helped him up and he slumped down on the sun warmed log.

"Want to wait for someone else to rescue you, David, or will I do?" Edie teased as she looked for a way to help him out of the water.

"Nah … I think you'll be fine," David answered back. She straddled the tree trunk and offered her arm as a life-line while he abandoned his tube. Next the two turned their attention to getting Rocky out of the water. Since he was the biggest of the four, they were especially careful to make sure their handholds were solid before they reached out to grab one out-stretched hand and then the other.

For a long while, the four of them just lay on the trunk of the tree, not talking. At last they could relax. They felt the water push against the tree and felt the whole huge trunk bob ever so slightly in the current. They felt the warmth of the sun melt away the chill of fear and they felt the creeping happiness that comes from knowing you have amazingly escaped a very dangerous situation.

"So shall we go on?" Rocky finally broke their silence.

"I can't. Take a look at my so-called lifesaver." Nick pointed to the deflated tube. "I saw it bounce against a broken stick over and over again and I think it just wore a hole through it."

"Are we just going to leave our tubes here?" asked David.

"I don't know how you plan to carry them through this maze of branches and then up the steep bank over there. And we're barefoot … I think I'm gonna be focusing on where I'm stepping, not on whether my tube is gonna make it. Besides we can come back when we've got some help from my dad." Edie had had enough river for one day. She was ready to get out of there and make her way home.

"Well, you know we're never supposed to leave our tubes. They're our life-preservers. Everybody says so. It's kinda like a rule," Rocky said with just a hint of teasing in his voice.

"And sometimes the best advice is to ignore all the advice," Edie shot back, her eyes sparkling with a new-found confidence in listening to that quiet inner voice.

"Okay, so what advice are we going to ignore trying to get out of here?" Rocky challenged, his own eyes twinkling with their verbal sparring.

"Like it or not, the advice we are going to ignore is that you have to wear shoes when you hike," Edie laughed.

The four teens picked their way through the branches to the place where the tree trunk was still attached to the riverbank. Edie led the way. She was eager to get back to the neighborhood, not only to get some shoes, but especially to thank Uncle Sol for rescuing them from disaster.

John 14:17-19, 25, 26

Theological Foundation: see p.230
Guide for Non-religious Settings: see p.259

Lilacs

Rocky rang the doorbell a second time. He waited; it wasn't like Uncle Sol to not answer the door on a Saturday morning. The envelope with Rocky's prom pictures slowly drooped to the teenager's side as he reluctantly turned to step down the stairs. "I really wanted to show Uncle Sol how good I looked in a tuxedo," he muttered to himself. He was just about to reach the bottom step when he heard the door open. Wheeling around, Rocky was surprised to see Hank, Uncle Sol's oldest son standing in the doorway.

"Hi there—Rocky, isn't it?" Rocky nodded that Hank was right. "You were looking for Dad, weren't you? We arrived last night and Gramps has taken our boys down to the lake. Anything I can do for you?"

"No … thanks … you're Hank, right?"

"Yup, that's me," answered Uncle Sol's son, who still looked like a well-trained athlete in his hooded sweatshirt and wind-pants.

"Uhhh … listen, I gotta thank you. Well actually, I guess it wasn't you, but Uncle Sol, I mean your dad. He loaned me your team jacket after I tore mine up. When coach saw it, he did a double-take." Unknowingly, Rocky imitated Coach's expression and Hank laughed out loud. "I was afraid he'd be really mad. He kinda glared at me and made me sit right behind him on the bus. After I told him what happened to my jacket, he just shook his head and then started to tell me stories about you and your team. It ended up being pretty cool. I only wore it that one day, until I had time to get a new one … but your dad rescued me … again. And I heard what a great team you guys had."

Hank smiled, "Dad called me and told me what he'd done with my jacket. I was glad it got used for a change instead of just sitting in the closet … Hey, that was a pretty good imitation of Coach, by the way."

Rocky smiled and was turning to leave when a thought crossed his mind and he just stopped. He looked up at Hank, "Hey, I … I … was just wondering … ya know Uncle Sol, I mean your dad … he's a pretty unique guy. Nobody's like him in this neighborhood. I don't think there's anybody like him anywhere. Sometimes me and my friends talk and we were just kinda wondering how'd he get to be that way? Was he always like this? Even as a little kid?"

Hank was quiet for a moment, clearly thinking about how to answer such an earnest question. "Rocky, you got a few minutes? I think I have something that will answer that question. I'll be right back." Within moments Hank reappeared at the door with a folder in his hand. He stepped right outside and gestured for Rocky to come sit down on the top step with him. The folder contained type-written poems and stories that Rocky could see as Hank sorted through them clearly looking for a specific paper.

"Ah, here it is. Dad wrote poems and stories for us kids when we were little. When we moved out for good after college Dad gave us each our own copy … but I know where he keeps the originals," Hank said with the same twinkle in his eye that Rocky had seen in Uncle Sol's. The stapled story's paper was yellowed with age. It had been handled so many times that even the holes made by the staples were enlarged, making the pages slip back and forth on each other.

"Read it. It won't take long, I've got time … in fact, if you don't mind, I'd like to read it out loud to you. It's been a long time since I looked at this, but I think there is a clue to answering your question."

"Sure, go ahead … I was comin' to visit Uncle Sol anyway … I got time." Rocky followed along as Hank started to read.

Marta and the Lilacs

"Mutti, Mutti, these are for you," little Marta held out her hands filled with lilacs. Her mother dropped to her knees.

"Marta, they are beautiful" and then she put her face right into the lilacs and took a deep breath.

"They smell so wonderful ... thank you, thank you." The mother gave her little girl a big hug.

Marta's mother didn't ask where she got the flowers. She knew that Marta had to have taken them from someone's bush because they had no lilacs at their home. They hardly had a home. They hardly had food. Marta's mother had to search very hard to find any food for her two children to eat. Marta never knew from one night to the next if there was going to be something for supper.

You see, they lived in Germany. At the end of World War II, Germany was in ruins. Buildings that had been destroyed remained piles of rubble. Roads were cleared so that trucks and jeeps could pass, but it was all very dangerous. Everything was wrecked, everything was dusty and dirty. No water came out of the faucets in their little apartment; there was no electricity and very little food and every one was discouraged. But Marta was only four, she was glad there were no more sounds of war; she could play with her friends outside now. One day jeeps and trucks rolled into her town. The soldiers wore uniforms she'd never seen and they spoke a language no one understood. Marta and all the children were frightened and the grown-ups were very worried ... but one day, the soldiers from America who walked the streets of her town started to hand out chocolate candies. You can imagine how wonderful chocolate tasted when you didn't have much to eat. She tried to get more than one piece so that she could share that with her mother and brother, but the soldier showed her one finger letting her know that she could only have one.

Marta saw the same soldiers every day for a while, but there was one who had the nicest smile and he always made sure that the bigger children did not shove her out of the way when the candy and gum appeared. Marta liked him a lot.

On the day she found the lilac bush with its flowers blooming she only wanted to take the flowers to her Mutti, but the very next day, she had another thought: she would take lilacs to her soldier friend. Marta had felt very brave collecting the flowers, but when she saw her soldier friend standing with the other soldiers near the jeeps, she suddenly felt very shy ... she hid the lilacs behind her back. She even thought about leaving, but her soldier friend saw her and smiled. He walked away from the small group of men he'd been talking with and came right over to Marta. When he reached her, he took off his helmet and knelt down so his little German friend didn't have to look up so high. He reached into his pocket and pulled out a candy bar just for her. Marta's eyes grew large. It was the biggest piece of chocolate she'd ever seen. Slowly Marta took her hands out from behind her back. The beautiful purple lilacs filled the space between them with color and their sweet distinctive smell.

Now it was the soldier's turn to have his eyes grow wide with surprise. If Marta could have understood English, she would have heard the American soldier say, "Oh my, I haven't seen lilacs since I left home in Maine." Marta held up the bouquet of lilacs to him—a gift. He slowly took it from her with a smile and then he handed her the chocolate bar—a gift in return.

When the soldier stood up he put the lilac in his shirt pocket. They waved to each other and that is the last she saw of him. The soldiers went away in their jeeps and trucks to another city. But Marta always remembered the lilacs that made everyone smile at a time when there wasn't much to smile about.

And the young soldier? Well, his unit got sent to another area and then another. He carried the lilac around until it wilted and he had to throw it away. Eventually he came home. When the next spring arrived and he saw lilacs everywhere, he remembered his little German friend. He remembered how beautiful that lilac she held out to him looked after so many months of ugliness. He made up his mind that he wanted to be like little Marta and bring something beautiful to the people around him, especially if their lives were not going very smoothly—just the way Marta had brought something beautiful to him when life wasn't very easy and he was far from home.

So that's what he did ... he found beautiful flowers along roadsides and brought them to his girl friend and his mother and the neighbor down the street who needed cheering up. He decided to do something every day to make the world a bit more beautiful. Sometimes it was with lilacs, sometimes with other flowers, sometimes it was with a smile and a kind word, sometimes it was with a helping hand but in one way or another he managed for all the years of his life to make the world a more beautiful place.

"That's Uncle Sol isn't it?" Rocky burst in as soon as Hank finished.

"Well, I don't know, Rocky. We always asked Dad if that was him and he wouldn't say one way or the other. He'd just say, 'Good story, huh?' And we were always left wondering."

"If it isn't a true story about him ... it's as good as true because that's just what he's like. I think he does wake up every day figuring out who he can be helpful to or who he can cheer up. He does make the world a more beautiful place ... look at this yard! He's amazing." Rocky's admiration for his elder neighbor and friend was clear.

"We all think he's pretty amazing," responded Hank. "We're especially lucky because he's our dad." As Hank was putting the story back in the folder, he noticed the envelope in Rocky's hand. "What ya' got there, Rocky?"

"Oh, just some pictures from the prom. I was gonna show Uncle Sol. He never sees me dressed up."

"Mind if I have a look?" Hank asked.

Rocky offered the envelope to Hank and started to tell him about all the kids in the pictures. That's where Uncle Sol found them as he and the grandsons came around the side of the house—Hank and Rocky sitting on the top steps talking and laughing. For the briefest moment, Uncle Sol thought, "There, I've handed it on … another generation of good neighbors in-the-making."

"Hey, Dad, Rocky and I have been getting to know each other. Boys, how'd you like the lake with Gramps?" The grandsons ran to their dad, exploding with tales of adventure at the lake.

Rocky jumped to the bottom of the stairs and called out to Uncle Sol, "Later!"

Uncle Sol smiled and responded with "You bet—and I wanna see those pictures myself later!" and nodded as he ushered his son and grandsons into the house for a late morning snack.

Matthew 28:16-20; Acts 1:4-8

Theological Foundation: see p.232
Guide for Non-religious Settings: see p.261

Appendix A
The Journey from a 'Telling Story' to a 'Reading Story' and Back Again…

Uncle Sol stories originated as 'telling stories' late on Saturday nights when the clock was ticking and I had discovered no suitable story for use in worship. Those long hours of preparation literally disappeared as the story unfolded in vivid detail in my mind. I would write down enough to capture the flow of the action and then simply 'tell' the story of what I had 'seen' happen in Uncle Sol's neighborhood the night before. In the worship service, during the 'children's message' where these tales were first heard, the children were always the intended audience. As they became familiar with Uncle Sol's neighborhood friends, the children wanted to know more about Uncle Sol—where he lived and when they could meet him. It was clear that Uncle Sol was a living, breathing person in their imaginations. The truth is that Uncle Sol was/is a living, breathing person in my imagination.

The wonder of storytelling is that the storyteller transfers what she/he imagines to the listener's imagination. When telling a story, sharing that moment with your listener, you can actually watch the creative image in your mind moving invisibly through the air into the creative imagination of your listener, a transfer that is nothing short of miraculous. For when you tell a story, there really is nothing between you and those who are listening; no books or pictures. Yet by mutual agreement, you come together for a time and mingle your minds. As the teller, you can see the interest in their eyes, their bodies leaning forward, engaged and waiting for the next words and images to emerge. It is a cooperative effort between the storyteller and the listeners. Together you create a shared experience of imaginative adventure.

These particular stories have been expanded into 'reading stories' by adding the detail I had envisioned in the first place. In order to return them to their 'original' form for use in worship or an abbreviated storytelling session, you as teacher or pastor must do a little work.

To begin, you need to be familiar with the story itself. Read it over several times until you have the sequence of the story well in mind. Then slow down and begin to imagine the whole story, scene by scene. Imagine what each child looks like, imagine Uncle Sol, imagine the yard or the hen house or the trees, imagine smells and sounds, tastes and colors. The more fully you imagine the setting and the characters, the more successful you will be at transferring what you are 'seeing and hearing' into the imaginations of your listeners. Pay attention to the dialog, but once you have a 'feel' for the characters and the action, let go of the need for 'accuracy' and just let them speak for themselves through you.

Practice 'telling' the story out loud. If you have a willing listening partner, have that person listen to you tell the story. As you tell the story, enter into it. Speak the tale as if you were an eye witness to the events; you are, in fact, an eye witness to what your imagination embodies for you and you can convey that to your listeners. If you are comfortable suggesting different characters by a slight change in your voice tones, by all means, do so. If you are comfortable making some of the gestures that would make the character come to life along with the voice tones, do so. All efforts to embody the characters bring a story to life and help transfer the images from your creative mind to the recipient's creative mind.

There is a great temptation to give the 'moral' of the story to children in worship or in a classroom setting. I can only encourage you to refrain. The Master Storyteller, Jesus, always let the story speak for itself and let people wonder at the many layers of meaning. It is no different here. Allow the story to touch the children (and adults ☺) where it can. For some it will speak volumes about the qualities of a relationship with God. For others it will simply be a story about a kind old neighbor and a kid like themselves. Either one will teach. Of course, you are free to use these in whatever ways meet your need as pastor or teacher. Enjoy the experience.

Appendix B
Theological Foundations for the Stories

Because I have an aversion to simply applying a single 'moral' or meaning to each of these stories, it seems important for you as the pastor, teacher, or parent to have a bit more background into my thinking about each one. One of my goals is to have everyone who uses these stories reflect theologically on the story's scriptural underpinnings. The questions that are provided are not scaled to any specific age. I simply hope these questions will prompt your questions or that you will adjust the questions to meet the specific age abilities of the ones with whom you are sharing these stories.

A Drop of Faith

I Corinthians 15:20-26
Matthew 28

Life after death, eternal life, and resurrection are all words and phrases familiar to Christians. But the reality of trusting what you cannot see and believing the promises of God … believing that Jesus is "the first fruits of those who have fallen asleep" … is as much a challenge for us as it was for the first followers. The ability to trust God in life and in death comes from knowing this God to be a God of love who rescues, who deeply cares about each unique human life, who has made the ultimate sacrifice on our behalf and knowing that reality personally.

At the point of life when we are utterly incapable of helping ourselves any longer; at the transition from this life to the life to come, believing is the power to let go into God's loving eternal embrace.

David, for all his mischievousness and self-reliance, calls on the one he believes he can count on to help him in his time of need. At that moment, hanging in the tree, David first tries to rely on his own strength to rescue himself from a desperate situation. When he is confronted with his inability to help himself, he calls upon Uncle Sol. His relationship with Uncle Sol is such that he believes his elder friend will be able to keep him safe even in the midst of trouble. It is only when Uncle Sol asks him to do what seems crazy that David balks and tries once again to save himself. Only the reliability of the relationship with Uncle Sol gives David the courage to utterly entrust himself to Uncle Sol's care by dropping from the branch to the arms he can only hope are there and ready to catch him.

Questions

1. Is Uncle Sol at fault for David's troubles? (Is God to blame for the circumstances of our lives?)
2. How does David get himself into trouble?
3. How is trusting God with our lives like David trusting Uncle Sol to catch him?
4. Why did it take courage for David to let go?
5. Why does it take courage to trust God with our lives?
6. How might we get to a point where we can trust God whom we cannot see as much as David trusts Uncle Sol?

Team Effort

1 Corinthians 12:4-11

St. Paul gives us such a clear picture of how God works in community. No one person is given all the skills, talents, wisdom or strength to do everything in the church. Each person is given a unique God-gift which is intended to enhance the life of the whole gathered community of God. When people recognize their distinctive God-gift and share it, wonderful things can happen which allow God's good news to spread far beyond the small group of people themselves.

Our society is a bit double-minded about community. We are staunchly protective of individual rights and, at the same time, we praise individuals who work together as a team in order to accomplish their goals. In truth, because our culture fosters the creation of individuals who seek the 'good of the individual' first, the development of a mindset that seeks the 'good of the community' is severely hindered. Christianity emerged out of a culture that valued community deeply. God as Father, Son and Spirit is the 'divine community' that provides the pattern for all other communities. This Trinitarian model colors everything about our faith, how we come to faith, how we remain in the faith. Relationship is at its core.

In this story, Uncle Sol helps the children discover their strength at problem-solving as they pool their unique contributions in a "dire" situation. As Uncle Sol points out, no one item each child shared could have resolved the crisis, but each thing working in concert with other bits and pieces the children brought made short work of it. Even the little sister who appeared to only be an in-the-way-nuisance played a crucial role. In God's kingdom, everyone has a distinctive place of importance. At the same time, everyone is part of something much larger that can only exist when each distinctive soul takes its place beside other distinctive souls for God's sake.

Questions

1. What was it Jenny wanted so much that she ignored her mother's rule? Could this problem have been avoided altogether? Why do some children ignore family rules in order to do something friends want? What problems can you see developing from such choices?
2. When Jenny's necklace drops into the storm drain, why are the friends unable to help her? Are the children work-

ing together or separately when they make all their suggestions? How does Uncle Sol help them work together?
3. Could you figure out what Uncle Sol was going to do with a kite, safety pins, and duct tape? How are those unrelated objects like people in a group? What made the completely unrelated objects valuable to Uncle Sol?
4. God makes each of us a unique individual like no one else on the planet. He also puts us in family groups and communities and states and countries. Why do you suppose God did that?
5. According to God's teachings found in the Bible, are we supposed to look out for ourselves or are we to look out for others? Why do you think God planned it that way?
6. God gives us unique gifts, God-gifts (you can find lists of such gifts in I Corinthians 12:7-11, 27-31; Romans 12:6-8) for use in the community of faith. Is there any use to having a God-gift if you are unwilling to share it with God's people? Why would God have us share our gifts? How is that like the children sharing their unique "gifts" with Uncle Sol for Jenny's sake?
7. What might God want to accomplish in the world through all the people he has given God-gifts to? Are you willing to share your unique God-gift? If you don't know what it is yet, are you willing to find out and then share it?

Kite Calamity

Genesis 3:1-7
Romans 5:12-19

The idea of original sin as disobedience to what God asks of us is an important concept for children and adults to grasp. Too many people teach that original sin means humans are just plain 'bad'. But Genesis 1:26-31 specifically tells us that when God created human beings, he blessed them and called all that he had created 'good'. The original sin that is transmitted from one generation to the next is simply and profoundly this: we have forgotten how to choose obedience to God's commands to love him with our whole heart, mind, soul and strength and to love our neighbors as ourselves. We have forgotten for so long that no one really knows how to be obedient in a way that lets us have the wide open relationship with God that Adam and Eve knew before the great disaster in the Garden.

Our open access to God was lost to us by our primordial parents' disobedience and the subsequent loss of memory on how to be in an obedient, loving relationship to our Maker continues to plague us. No amount of "work" or sacrifices or "right practices of prayer" or anything else on our part could repair the breach between us and our Creator. But it is critical to remember our Trinitarian understanding of God. Our Maker chose to help us when we couldn't help ourselves. He came to us in a form we could understand, the form of a human—Jesus. And Jesus did what no human, including Adam,had been able to do: he was completely obedient to God, because he was God. And he was also a man, a man filled with the power of God's Spirit. By his willing obedience to death, he became the bridge over the breach for us all.

In the story, Julie experiences the freedom of unmerited grace. Her disobedience to the rules, with its disastrous effects, has a lasting impact on her life. Her parents want to make sure she understands the severity of disobeying the rules and they will not relent in their requirement that she repay them. After allowing her to live with the reality of her poor choice for a while, Uncle Sol intervenes. She doesn't deserve it. He acknowledges that, but he chooses with her parents' permission to help set her free from an obligation from which she is unable to free herself.

Questions

1. How is Julie leading the other children astray? Why did she do that?
2. How do we justify decisions we make that might be contrary to the rules we have been given?

3. How did Eve justify her decision to eat of the forbidden fruit? (Gen. 3.13)
4. What happened to Eve and Adam? (see Genesis 3.16-23)
5. What allowed Julie to return to her usual childhood pastimes?
6. Why do you suppose Uncle Sol chose to help Julie?
7. What allows human beings to now be in a right relationship with God? (see Romans 5.12-19 ... use two or three versions of the Bible to help you see the scope of Paul's thinking. The Message by Eugene Peterson is helpful here for students and for their teachers.)
8. What was Julie's response to Uncle Sol's gift? Why did she respond this way?
9. What tends to be the response to God's free gift of reconciliation among 'church kids'? What would it take for 'church kids' to respond like Julie to God's gift in Jesus Christ?

Lemonade Wisdom

Matthew 13: 13-17

This particular passage from Matthew quoting Isaiah communicates a harshness about God that is mystifying in our current context. You are encouraged to look at a biblical commentary or two on this passage because they can be very helpful. Even though these verses are perplexing, there is truth here that is hard to deny. Receptivity to new teaching, new ways of understanding something that we have always known requires us to be attentive, open. When people have made up their minds about the correctness of their position about God or human beings or anything else, all evidence to the contrary washes over them, leaving them untouched. This is why Jesus is quick to point out to his disciples that their own eyes and ears are blessed, having been freed to really see the new thing which God is doing for the world through Jesus' presence.

The well-worn quote, "People have been inoculated with just enough Christianity to be immune to it," applies to far too many church-goers in our own time. It creates calloused hearts that miss the wonder of God's presence in the present moment. Only by pealing back that callous through story or "en-acted parables" is there hope of waking up a sleepy, benumbed heart and changing it into a potentially receptive heart. Jesus used parables to teach, to awaken, to direct and to correct ideas about God and what God requires of us. The method is just as valuable today.

In this particular story, Edie has a "calloused heart". She is a "know it all". She acts as though she wants to gain new knowledge from Uncle Sol, but in reality she only wants to show off to Uncle Sol all that she already knows. That is when Uncle Sol takes to a rather drastic measure to teach his young neighbor a very important lesson on receptivity.

Questions

1. What was Edie's problem? Even though she asked for Uncle Sol's help, from what you could tell, did she really want it?
2. How could Uncle Sol teach someone who already seemed to know all the answers?
3. Do you think Uncle Sol's method was a bit drastic? Why or why not? What other ways might Uncle Sol have tried to explain things to Edie?
4. How is Edie's misplaced self-assuredness similar to our way of thinking we know all about God? In what ways do children and grown-ups who go to church all the time make similar mistakes like Edie, thinking they know all they need to know about God and their relationship to him?
5. Jesus told stories to sneak in under people's already formed ideas about God in order to teach them very important new lessons about God's ways. What ways would Jesus need to use to get your attention right now? Music? Videos? Video games? What? How might that help?

6. How can you remain open to God's voice in your every day life? How can you keep yourself open to discovering what God wants you to do with your life?

Inner Change

Mark 9:2-13

At the Transfiguration of Jesus, for a moment in time the three disciples saw the glory of God shining in and through their rabbi. It was a startling, unimaginable event that erased any rational thought from the minds of Jesus' friends. They experienced the unthinkable: they saw God-presence in a person and that person happened to be their teacher and friend. Jesus promised his followers, upon his resurrection, that God's Spirit would be with them and in some remarkable way would also be in them. After Pentecost, when the Holy Spirit rushed down upon them as a great wind, tongues of fire danced about their heads and seemed to rest on each of them—that is when the reality of Jesus' words came home to roost. Pentecost is when they were filled with God's Spirit and the whole world changed for them. Each disciple was forever changed. Courage, strength, grace, wisdom, and love were among the qualities that flowed out from them, reminiscent of their master. They began to look and act more like their Risen Lord each day. This has been a sign of followers of Christ ever since.

The presence of God's Spirit inside each believing heart awakens character qualities that lie dormant until enlivened by that special advent. Trying to describe such a time in a Christ-follower's life in story form presented a real challenge. Alice's tragedy had scarred her deeply and yet with the experienced reality of care she had already known at her church, she was receptive to Uncle Sol's gentle message. Children and adults need to hear and experience repeatedly that they are treasured if they are to thrive. Alice's shy nature and her isolation made it particularly important for Uncle Sol to gently draw connections for her that could help her see the world in a new way … could in a real sense transform her way of seeing. It allowed her to see that she was treasured in a deep, spiritual way. No human will be transfigured as Jesus was on that day on the mountain, but people can be transformed by God's love here and now.

Questions

1. If you were one of the neighborhood kids who knew Alice, how might you react to her silence and unwillingness to play? What if you hadn't heard her tragic story? Would that change how you might treat her?
2. Why do you think Alice liked the kind of stories she did?
3. How did Uncle Sol help Alice see herself differently?
4. If Alice had not been going to church, would Uncle Sol's words about God have been as effective? How can being part of a church help us when tragic things happen to us? How does God work through the church to change people's lives?
5. What evidence do we have that God changes people? What evidence did Uncle Sol see in Alice? What might Uncle Sol look for in Alice's relationships and behavior in the weeks and months ahead?
6. How can you and your church family show God's love to children and adults in your midst who go through very difficult times?

A New Home for Christmas

John 1:10-13; John 3:16; Gal 3:26-29

Belonging—it is such a crucial hunger in the human heart. We want to belong, to feel a part of, to be with others. God places that need for community in the fabric of human hearts. Our very survival depends upon our belonging to our families at birth and from there it extends to larger and larger groups. In the mobile society in which we live, the longing for belonging often goes unsatisfied for years for those who move into a new area. Churches provide a perfect place for people who have no close connections in a community to find a ready-made "family". Yet more often than Christians would like to admit, people who regularly attend church have forgotten what it feels like to be on the outside looking in. The need to extend ourselves to the one who is seeking welcome is simply acting in the same manner as the Good Shepherd who went after the lost sheep.

Nick has moved into Uncle Sol's neighborhood and he is very lonely. This loneliness is particularly accentuated at Christmas time. During the holidays, the emotionally-laden traditions are particularly painful when observed through the window panes of grieving. Nick was grieving all that he had left behind in his old neighborhood and he had not yet found any way to belong in his new neighborhood. Enter Uncle Sol who is very observant and always pro-active when it comes to children. He helped organize the neighborhood children into a welcoming committee which turned Nick's whole life around.

Extending a welcoming hand to newcomers takes courage on the part of those who already belong to a group. There is risk involved because one does not know the outcome of offering the hand of friendship. Hopefully this story will prompt conversations with your students about the importance of reaching out to the stranger—the new kid on the block.

Questions

1. Where do you feel like you belong? Your family? Your school? Your neighborhood? Your sports team? Your church? Have you always been in this community or did you move here from somewhere else?
2. Have you ever felt like Nick? Have you ever felt like an outsider and that there was no way to become an insider? Were you able to change that? What did you do?

3. Have you ever had a new kid try to join a group you were in? How did you react to the new person? Did you try to help that person feel comfortable or did you try to ignore them?
4. Should the new person have to do all the work of trying to join a group or should an existing group try to help the new person find a way to belong?
5. How does God make people feel like they are important to him? Does God expect people to do all the work of finding him or did God go out of his way to help people get back in touch with him? How did he do that?
6. What is the most important message of Jesus' birth? How did God show that he loved people and wanted them to belong to God's family?
7. What are the ways you can help new kids and adults become part of the church family where you belong? If you are among the new ones to your church community, what helped you feel like you belonged? What could be done to help that happen even better?
8. God uses the church to help the whole world understand that it belongs to God's family. How might your church be part of God's message to the town or city where you live?

An Unexpected Flower

Ephesians 2.7-10
Luke 15.4-7

God's grace is a free gift, undeserved, impossible to earn. Recognizing our need for God's gracious presence in our lives is the first evidence that God's activating Spirit is already busy at work in our hearts. St. Paul makes explicit the gift nature of God's activity in all human life.

"Now God has us where he wants us, with all the time in this world and the next to shower grace and kindness upon us in Christ Jesus. Saving is all his idea, and all his work. All we do is trust him enough to let him do it. It's God's gift from start to finish! We don't play the major role. If we did, we'd probably go around bragging that we'd done the whole thing! No, we neither make nor save ourselves. God does both the making and saving. He creates each of us by Christ Jesus to join him in the work he does, the good work he has gotten ready for us to do, work we had better be doing." Ephesians 2:7-10 (The Message)

Rocky has moved into the neighborhood in the midst of a tumultuous time in his own life. He does not have the emotional maturity to handle all the chaotic feelings and thoughts that come with his loss. He takes it out on anyone who comes near to him, including Uncle Sol. When he reaches his breaking point he does the unthinkable. He attacks his neighbor's garden with a vengeance. He faces up to his wrong-doing, but he can't face up to Uncle Sol. However Uncle Sol is not one to give up on anyone. He offers welcome repeatedly and finally wears down Rocky's resistance. The ensuing confession, repentance and reconciliation give a window into the way that God's grace works in our own lives. Grieving in good ways and poor ways, wrong-doing, remorse, confession, reconciliation, and grace are all avenues to be explored through this story.

Questions

1. Why was Rocky so angry? Would you be under those circumstances? What is the difference between sorrow and anger? Why might it be important to recognize that sorrow and anger can get mixed up?
2. Are there good ways to show anger and poor ways to show anger? How do you show anger that is a 'good' way?
3. Why do you think Rocky begins to care about what Uncle Sol thinks?
4. Could you be like Uncle Sol and continue to show kindness even when the person you are showing kindness to treats you like Rocky treated Uncle Sol?

5. Why was it important to Uncle Sol to keep treating Rocky so kindly even with Rocky's bad attitude? What difference did it make over time?
6. How does God treat us when we have made bad choices? Does God ever give up on changing people's hearts? What makes you say that?
7. Rocky finally talks with Uncle Sol. Rocky tells Uncle Sol what he did, he tells his elderly neighbor why he did it, and then he repeats his apology to which Uncle Sol replies, "I forgave you the first time." In Christian practice it is called confession, repentance and absolution. Why is it important to 'confess' and express remorse when you've done something to wrong another person?
8. Did Rocky 'earn' Uncle Sol's forgiveness and invitation to come to his home often? How is Uncle Sol's offering of welcome to Rocky like God's grace offered to us?
9. What possibilities opened up for Rocky once he accepted Uncle Sol's invitation? What possibilities open up to people who accept God's gift of grace in their own lives?
10. How is Rocky himself 'the unexpected flower'?

Secret Artist

Matthew 2:1-12
Luke 2:1-19

Christmas traditions are so integral to our celebration of Jesus' birth that we can hardly think of Christmas without thinking of wreathes and decorated trees, twinkling lights and special cookies, stockings and Santa Claus. Try as we might to put a more holy spin on the holiday in our homes, the cultural observance of Christmas has a huge influence on all of us. The history of the manger scenes or crèche goes back to St. Francis who is said to have staged the first live Nativity scene in Greccio, Italy 1223. His purpose was to turn people's hearts away from the secular materialism of his own day and return them to a proper focus on Christ. The Pope gave his blessing to Francis' nativity scene and the practice became extremely popular throughout Christendom. Eventually, statues replaced the live scenes in village displays. Ultimately this shift was the origin of our own home nativity scenes.

Uncle Sol has his own Christmas traditions which include setting up a nativity scene, but this year a child in the neighborhood believes he needs to add to his collection. The gift of time and thoughtful planning that is represented in the gift-a-night hints at the giver's deeper understanding of Jesus' birth. Uncle Sol's adult children are aware that their father is quite special in his own right, that he daily lives the message of Christmas in the neighborhood. Perhaps a discussion about the purpose of gifts and the ways to receive gifts no matter what they are could be part of your Christmas conversation with your students.

Questions

1. What makes Christmas so special to you?
2. What made this Christmas so special for Uncle Sol?
3. Did Uncle Sol think it was a problem to have two nativity scenes?
4. Have you ever been given something that you already have? What was your reaction? Was it like or unlike Uncle Sol's reaction?
5. Why do we give gifts on Christmas? Would Christmas still be Christmas if no gifts were given?
6. What was God's gift to the world? Do you think people recognized how special that gift was at first? Do you think people recognize how important and special that first Christmas gift is today?
7. You might have heard the phrase, "Be a cheerful giver". Have you ever heard the phrase, "Be a cheerful receiver"? What difference might that make to someone who gives you a gift? What difference might that make to you when you give a gift to someone?
8. What does it mean in the story to say that " … the real Christ Child was very much alive in their father's heart

and was still bringing joy to the world one family at a time…"? What lets us know that Jesus Christ is alive in someone's heart? Is that true about your heart?

Trusting the Clues

John 14:1-14

When Jesus says, "I am the way, the truth and the life. No one comes to the Father except through me," he opens us up to a broader understanding of his mission than we might first suspect. After all, we know that a 'way' is a road or a path that gets us from one place to another. So in that sense, Jesus does help us move from where we are currently separated from God for all kinds of reasons to a point where we are not separated from God any longer. We also know that "way" is a method of doing something. In that respect, watching Jesus live his life in relation to his disciples, the crowds, or the individual soul he encounters becomes a guide for our way of being in relationship with others.

There are those who voice concern that Christianity is just too exclusive and quote this passage to prove their point. If we take the understanding of "way" as just described, it would make sense that Jesus would make this claim. Just as Will was the only "way" to Uncle Sol because he knew how to get from the chestnut tree to the tree house, so Jesus really is the only one who knows how to get to the Father. People are free to wander and undoubtedly some, in their fervent search for God, will stumble upon the Creator of the Universe. (It is important for all Christ-followers to remember that Jesus does not condemn those who are searching, but invites them to look more closely at the way he offers. We must imitate his method of invitation, not condemnation to those who are outside the fellowship of faith.) However, for sheer ease of reaching the goal of God, Jesus provides the surest way because he knows how to get us to that relationship.

In the second meaning of "way", Jesus' behavior models for us the kind of life that brings us into relationship with the Father. It is just easier to learn if we have a real live example. Jesus' life gives his followers exactly that kind of live model.

When a person embodies the "way, the truth, and the life," it is much easier to figure out what to do. We do what that person does. We have a model and, in Jesus, we have both the model and the means for imitating that model. Such an abstract concept is not an easy one to communicate to young children. That is why I wrote this story. For young children it might be important to just anchor the basic premise of the story to Jesus' mission in the world.

Questions

1. Did you think that it was clever of Uncle Sol to have Will be the clue?
2. Which is easier to follow: directions on paper or to follow a person who knows where she is going?
3. How is Jesus' leading us to the Father like Will leading the children to Uncle Sol in the tree house?

For older students, conversations could focus more on Jesus as the "way"

1. How do you learn best? Which would be more useful for the vast majority of people learning a new skill: reading about how to do it or having a person who knows the skill well actually show you and guide you in the way to perform the skill? What is the advantage of having a real live person be your on-the-spot instructor?
2. How is Jesus our "on-the-spot" instructor in opening up a relationship with God?
3. Do you think Will got discouraged when the rest of the kids ignored him? What did Uncle Sol tell Will he could say when anyone talked to him while he was under the chestnut tree? What allowed Edie to actually be the first one to the tree house? What did she actually say to Will?

4. How is Edie's willingness to follow Will a key component to understanding Jesus' statement, "I am the way, the truth and the life"?
5. Have you figured out how Jesus is the "way" in your life? What more information do you need to understand Jesus' point for your own spiritual growth?

Seeing the Truth

1 Samuel 16.7
Psalm 139
Matthew 15:10-20

The old adage, "Seeing is believing," can still be heard bantered around when people want proof of something they have a hard time accepting as true. In the realm of religious faith, seeing with one's eyes does not necessarily give a person accurate data for understanding the ways of God. When Samuel was told by God to anoint the next king of Israel, he traveled to Bethlehem to the home of Jesse as he had been directed. Jesse brought out his sons; tall, handsome, their exterior presentation was kingly in every way. Even Samuel was caught by their outward appearance. However, God pressed his prophet to anoint God's choice among the sons of Jesse. Only when the father was questioned again did he mention his youngest son who was out in the field with the sheep. David was young, so while Samuel could see potential, he wondered at the choice. God reminded Samuel that he sees into the heart of the human being where the true character of the individual is clearly visible. It is the heart turned toward God that pleases our Creator.

How do we 'see' character? The actual evidence of character shows itself in behavior, but the behavior originates in the heart. Jesus clearly said that what comes out of a man's heart is what gives evidence of the man's character. William Barclay, British New Testament scholar wrote, "What matters to God is not so much how we act, but why we act; not so much what we actually do, but what we wish in our heart of hearts to do." (pg. 119, Gospel of Matthew, Volume 2) Additionally, Psalm 139 is particularly expansive in its revelation about the ways God sees each unique human creation. Helping a child understand that God sees us for who we are, beyond all our pretensions, is important. An equally critical lesson is that though God knows our intimate secrets, God does not reject us, but rather gave himself up for us all.

To bring this idea of God-seeing-into-the-heart-of-each-human down to a level that a child could grasp, a chapter from the book on pet ownership seemed helpful. We know from other stories that Uncle Sol has a finely tuned ability to "see" beyond appearances, a gift he regularly uses to good advantage in his neighborhood. Nick finds such ability something he wants to cultivate after he hears Uncle Sol's explanation of how he "sees".

Questions

1. What character qualities do you see in Nick? What kind of a teen is he?
2. What character qualities do you see in Uncle Sol? What kind of a neighbor is he?
3. What makes it possible for you to determine what character qualities these two have?
4. What was Uncle Sol looking for in Kristy?
5. Why do you suppose Jesus said that "the eye is the lamp of the body" (Matthew 6:22)? What did he mean by that?
6. Do you ever look into people's eyes to see what they really mean? Are you able to tell what is going on inside a person by looking into their eyes?
7. Why does it matter to God that we don't get stuck on outward appearances of other people?
8. Why should it matter to us that God does not get stuck on outward appearances?
9. Re-read 1 Samuel 16:7. Then read Psalm 139. What is God's attitude toward human beings? Is it a relief that

God can "see" our inward being and is free from being caught by our external appearances? Why? Why not?
10. How might it change the way you relate to others knowing that God sees the inner workings of your heart?

The Boy Who Would Be King

Mark 10:35-45

Being a leader of people usually requires some wielding of a highly valued commodity in our culture: power. Power can be derived from economic sources and status or it can be obtained by force—either police/military force or a personal show of greater physical strength. It can also come from a combination of the two. From the point of view of 'the world', there is consistency across time and cultures that the sources of power are found in some blend of money and force.

What stands in contrast to these ideas is the teaching of Jesus on power sources. He turns conventional wisdom upside down. The strong are those who are 'weak'. The leader is the one who chooses to serve. Not the proud but the humble will get the nod. It does not make sense at all if one seeks conventional advice on sources of leadership power.

Power in the realm of God is a very different kind of power. It looks like the human is 'making' all the effort. Yet if you talk to the human who has placed his or her trust in God, you hear a different story. You hear how God is providing the power and the strength and the wisdom to do whatever is being accomplished. When a follower of Jesus admits to being weak and turns to God for strength, a new kind of strength comes through God's Spirit. When a follower of Jesus chooses to serve others like Jesus taught, people are drawn to the servant and the servant becomes a leader. Humility opens the door for boasting not in one's achievements, but in God's gracious gifts.

This is the kind of leadership about which Uncle Sol wants to instruct the boys. He uses the illustration of Mother Teresa because he is fairly confident that they might have heard her name. She also embodies this God-kind-of-power in her own life and work. Remarkable servants of God who have a Kingdom-of-God concept of power have made an enormous impact on the world. The vast majority remain nameless to us, but known to God. A few, like Mother Teresa, are a gift to all Christ-followers because in her we see again the truth of Jesus' mission in the world. His means of exercising power, wherever he is given free rein in someone's heart, transforms the harshness of the world into pockets of relief and hope.

Questions

1. Why did David think that being a king would make a person the most powerful ruler in the world?
2. Why did Jon think that having the most money would make a person the most powerful person in the world?
3. What do you think?
4. Why does Uncle Sol think it is important to correct the boys' thinking about real leadership?
5. Have good, long lasting changes happened for villages or nations where money or military force is the basis for the power the leaders have? Can you think of any examples from history? From current events?
6. What does Jesus teach about leadership?
7. How does the story of Agnes—Mother Teresa—point out the truth of Jesus' teaching?
8. How can you prepare yourself to be a leader like Mother Teresa or St. Francis or like any of Jesus' other disciples who have led people in his way?

The Sliding Hill

Acts 10:34ff

To be chosen as the leader is a much coveted honor among children which does not vanish when we become adults. Being chosen marks us as unique and special and worthy in the chooser's eyes. When Peter began to speak to the large gathering of people at Cornelius' home he began by acknowledging his awareness that God was doing something very new by extending the welcome to non-Jews. This was a transforming moment for Peter and for the emerging church. For generations Jews had known they had been chosen by God. They referred to themselves as the Chosen People. Their relationship with the Creator of the Universe was unique. They had experienced it as a blessing to be sure, but they had also experienced the challenging part of being God's special people. What they discovered is that being 'chosen' carried with it great responsibility. They mistakenly believed that being chosen by God as his special people meant they had special privileges over all others. That error in their thinking was the downfall of the People of Israel on more than one occasion. God was very clear to Abraham that he was being blessed in order to be a blessing to the nations. Peter, in a moment of Holy Spirit insight, understood that "God does not show favoritism but accepts people from every nation who fear him and do what is right."

These important ideas, that God shows no favoritism and that being chosen means responsibility not privilege, are the basis for this story about Edie's role as 'Protector' of the little children on the sliding hill. Edie is selected by Uncle Sol to be this season's 'protector'. She handles her job very well until conditions change and she decides to assert privilege over responsibility. Uncle Sol is quick to point out the error of her thinking when he discovers the problem. He is equally swift to forgive her and offer Edie another chance to understand her chosen status as one of deep responsibility instead of self-centered privilege.

Questions

1. What makes Uncle Sol's backyard such a special place in the neighborhood?
2. Does Uncle Sol have favorites? If you answer 'yes' what marks Uncle Sol's favorite children? If you answer 'no' why does Uncle Sol choose certain children for special roles in his backyard?
3. If Uncle Sol chooses you, what is expected of you?
4. How did Edie respond to her 'job'?
5. What decision got Edie into trouble? Why did she do it? Why was Uncle Sol disappointed in her?
6. How did Uncle Sol help Edie set things right?
7. How would you have felt if you had been Edie? One of the children she sent away? Uncle Sol?
8. God chose "the Children of Israel" to be a special 'protector' for all the people on earth. Why would God be unhappy when the children of Israel did not follow his commandments? How is that like Uncle Sol being unhappy with Edie when she didn't follow his rules?
9. Jesus' disciple Peter thought that he was only supposed to talk to the Jews about Jesus. What made him realize that God wanted him to talk to all people about Jesus (be sure to review Acts 10)? How is that like Edie being reminded that Uncle Sol's backyard was for everyone? How is it different?
10. Peter's new knowledge of God, given to him through the Holy Spirit because of his special relationship with Jesus, was to be shared with all people. How are we to carry on Peter's work in our own time and in our own places?

Patina Sisters

Psalm 25:1-9

We are reluctant to describe as 'sin' the harmful actions we see daily among family members, neighbors, government officials or healthcare workers to name a few. 'Sin' has such a large and overbearing presence in our minds that we will do all kinds of mental gymnastics to avoid being called "Sinner." Yet if we understood the origins or the word in Greek we might be a little less affronted by its stark accusations. The most frequently used word for "sin" in the New Testament is *hamartia*, an archery term which means, "missing the mark." There can be little doubt that when we think of God's high and holy standard for what is right in the ways we live in relationship to him, our fellow creatures and the planet, we are wide of the mark. Sometimes we miss the target completely.

While it is much easier to think in terms of other people being 'miserable sinners', we have a much more difficult time assigning that label to ourselves. And even if we can admit to ourselves that we may fall into that category of unregenerate human beings, we certainly find it grating to have someone else label our actions or behavior as sinful.

Naming ourselves as sinners is an important first step to opening up lines of communication with God and with each other. The mindless actions of a sister that hurt a little brother's developing conscience with her angry outbursts clearly missed God's high standard. The careless word that wounds so deeply that a sister carries the scars for decades is another sign that God's high and holy standard of how people are to treat one another was missed. It is little wonder that the psalmist asked God to forgive the sins of his youth. We can only pray that as we mature, we focus more carefully on the target of God's standard even as we rely on God's gracious love to cover over those sins.

In this particular story, sibling scuffles are the focal point. Growing up, sharing space, sharing parental attention is always challenging the minute more than one child is present in the family. Will has discovered to his dismay that his little sisters are as clever as they are adept at annoying him. In his attempts to fight back, he manages to get himself into even more trouble. He feels keenly the injustice of it all and wishes they would simply disappear. When he plants a rock in Uncle Sol's picket fence, he inadvertently invites Uncle Sol to help sort out his personal crisis. Conversations about the challenges of siblings, forgiveness and love in a family are all possibilities with this story.

Questions

1. Why do you think it is so difficult for Will to do what his mother wants him to do with his sisters: love them and forgive them?
2. How does Will's behavior miss the target of God's high and holy standard of behavior? How do his sisters miss the target of God's standard? Do you think either Will or his sisters would think of themselves as sinners?
3. What do you think is the point that Uncle Sol is trying to make by referring to the table and the tool box? If a person isn't perfect in behavior, does God give up on that person? Are we supposed to give up on that person?
4. The Psalmist David wrote, "Remember, O Lord, your great mercy and love, for they are from of old. Remember not the sins of my youth and my rebellious ways; according to your love remember me for you are good, O Lord." Psalm 25:6,7 What gives us the confidence not to give up on ourselves or God's love for us if we do fall short of God's target of high and holy standards of behavior?
5. How can brothers and sisters learn to live together peacefully? What lessons from Jesus' teaching about loving one another would be helpful to apply at home?

An Energetic Word

John 1:1-18

We are such concrete thinkers. Our scientific way of seeing the world has us focus almost exclusively on the material. If we can see something, touch it, manipulate it—whatever "it" is—then we know it is "real." While we do not completely dismiss it if we cannot handle it in some way, we are certainly more cautious with claims about "its" reality if we cannot see it and easily prove its existence.

Ancient thinkers had a different way of understanding 'reality'. They readily accepted the world they could see, touch, taste and manipulate but they were equally confident of the world they could not see. The sweeping passage opening John's Gospel captures the way Christians are to understand the action of the Almighty, Invisible God. John is consistent with the entire biblical narrative when he states that God's active agent is God's Word. God utters a word and "it" happens. Creation occurs only when God speaks. John's gospel carefully lays out the case for this Word-of-God-in-action to be understood as none other than Jesus himself. God speaks and we see Jesus. Jesus tells us that when we see him we see the Father.

These are difficult ideas to communicate to children. The use of Jenny's dream to help children imagine words actually having power to accomplish what they say seems useful. Uncle Sol is able to use Jenny's dream as a teaching moment which is this writer's intention for you.

Questions

1. Have you ever had a dream like Jenny's where you were almost convinced it was true?
2. Would you like your words to pop out of your mouth and do what you said just like Jenny's words did? What could be the good part about that happening? What could be the bad part about that happening?
3. In the dream there was no difference between Jenny and the way her words looked and acted. How do the words we speak every day reflect who we really are inside?
4. Jesus said that what comes out of a person, out of that person's mouth, shows us what the person is really like (Matthew 15:10-20). Our words let people know who we really are. In a way, our words look just like us when they are out and about in the world. People will decide about our character because of our words. How careful are you

with the words you use? Are you careful with the words you use at your home? At school? At church? At sporting events? At theater productions? In restaurants? Everywhere?
5. God spoke and the universe was created. When you look at the stars and the trees and the oceans and animals and people, what can you tell about God?
6. What can I tell about you by the words you speak? Are your words going to point me toward God or away from God?

The Borrowed Easter Egg

Mark 16

Easter is the reason there are Christians in the world today. Without the resurrection of Jesus, nothing he said makes any sense. For the only proof that he lived up to all the claims he made about himself was, in fact, his resurrection from the dead. From the moment Mary Magdalene reported finding the empty tomb all the way to the present day many hearing the resurrection story scoff and say "It just can't be true." We are asked to believe something that cannot be seen, that cannot be proven by replication, which had not happened before in the history of the world and has not happened since.

Finding ways to communicate this staggering reality has been an ongoing effort for the past 2000 years. Early Christians looked for things around them to use as metaphors for this most miraculous event. The caterpillar that metamorphosed into a lovely butterfly after looking quite dead in its cocoon was quickly commandeered as one such example. The egg was another. It looked "dead" but then life emerged from it as Jesus had emerged from the tomb. There are many more symbols that were discovered and utilized as teaching tools to communicate God's great victory over death. Many of our customs and our symbols surrounding Easter are accretions from different cultures that Christianity encountered as it spread from people group to people group. Christianity has never been afraid of "baptizing" such symbols and customs if it helped to spread the good news.

Uncle Sol's Easter Egg Hunt is a custom that dates back hundreds of years and is probably pre-Christian. The egg has been a symbol of new life for millennia, but as Uncle Sol points out to the children, it is a thoroughly Christian symbol for the resurrection of Jesus. In addition to being a way to talk about the resurrection of Jesus, the story itself could prompt many conversations about honesty, "borrowing", or consequences for poor decisions—for starters.

Questions

1. What happened to Jesus that first Easter?
2. Why is it so hard to find ways to talk about the resurrection of Jesus?
3. Jesus told the disciple Thomas, "Because you have seen me, you have believed; blessed are those who have not seen and yet have believed." (John 20:29) What symbol did Uncle Sol use to teach the children about the Resurrection of Jesus?
4. Do you think it is a useful symbol for understanding Easter?
5. What would help you understand Easter better?

and for character development…

6. What about Will's decision to "borrow" an egg from his neighbor's chicken coop? Was this a good or a bad decision? How did Will make taking the egg from Mr. Koth's chicken seem 'okay'?
7. What was another way Will might have gotten an egg?
8. Why do you think Will was so determined to do the whole Easter egg coloring tradition by himself?
9. Do you think Will's pride had anything to do with his decisions? Does pride make a person more at risk of making poor decisions?

10. Do you think Will's apology was enough or do you think it was a good idea for Mr. Koth accept Will's offer to clean the chicken coop?
11. Does it make sense to show by words and actions that someone is sorry for hurting another? Are words enough? Are actions enough?

Weed Seeds

Mark 12:28-34

The commandments of God really can be summed up very quickly in four words. "Love God, love others." If we have more than a nodding acquaintance with the New Testament, we have been exposed to what the New Testament writers understand as love. Beyond any idea of love as a 'warm-happy feeling', the biblical idea of love is defined by the way it shows itself in a person's life. Evidence of a loving heart includes patience, kindness, humble attitudes, truthfulness, faithfulness, a cheerful heart, generosity, hospitality and the like. If we can show this kind of behavior toward others, we are already demonstrating love to God. Jesus clearly commands us to love one another the way he loves us. This included the self-sacrificing part. The message of loving God and neighbor with our entire being is consistent throughout Jesus' ministry.

We often forget that it is the countless small acts of love that add up to a life of loving care for others in the style that God asks of us. In this particular story we find Alice busy trying to show her love for others by planting weed seeds which she regarded as beautiful in each friend's garden. Clearly the children who observed her efforts interpreted what they saw quite differently from what Alice intended. That, too, is a common occurrence. People intend one loving action and recipients do not experience it as love at all. Giving and receiving love is not as easy as one might think. God gave his love to us by sending us his son Jesus and the world has been quite divided as to whether this was a loving gift ever since it happened. That must not deter us from seeking to live out the life of love as outlined in 1 Corinthians, Romans and other places in scripture.

Helping children form the foundations of a life of loving God and loving others is a key part of educating young disciples. Giving students opportunities to demonstrate their growing capacity to be kind, patient, generous, self-controlled, peaceful, faithful and joyful is an on-going task of the church community.

Questions

1. Alice found some seeds that captured her imagination. Her 'sailing seeds' were supposed to be a gift to her neighbors. Why did some of the children think they were not a proper gift?
2. What is the best way to avoid confusion about what a person is doing? When Edie yelled to Uncle Sol to come outside to see what Alice was doing, was she doing that to be mean to Alice? How was Edie trying to show love? For whom? Might Edie have accomplished this in a little better way? How?
3. How did Uncle Sol show that he was a good 'gift-receiver'? What ways did Uncle Sol show love to Alice in front of all the children?
4. How is Uncle Sol's love like the love Jesus tells us we are supposed to have for each other?
5. What important lesson did Uncle Sol learn about loving God? Can we safely separate loving God and loving others? Are we missing something important if we only do half of what Jesus asks us to do by just loving God or just loving other people?
6. How are you doing at following Jesus' commandment to love God and love others? Which is easier? Why? What can you do to work on the harder one?

Lessons in Freezing

Luke 13:31-35

Ignoring God-given directives—the Children of Israel were as famous for that as they were for being given the commands from God in the first place. The Old Testament is filled with stories of God reaching out to this people with covenant arrangements designed to bless their lives. The one requirement was that they were to follow God's commands. How difficult they found that one condition for blessing! In their own minds, making allowances for changing circumstances made sense. God's rules could not apply under this situation could they? Such self-justifying reasoning always got the Children of Israel into trouble. Selective observance of God's rules was not part of God's instruction to his people. Though they continually failed to meet their part of the agreement, to worship God alone above all other gods, God did not give up on them. In the passage which prompted this story, Jesus is lamenting the unwillingness of his countrymen to embrace him and his message from God the Father. He draws the connection between himself and the long procession of prophets that preceded him. He speaks of his deep desire to protect his people and their utter blindness to his offer. Such offers are still extended to God's people.

In the story, Rocky was given clear warning of the dangers he would face if he ventured out on the old ice. Unfortunately, Rocky was so sure that he understood the nature of frozen water and ice that when the early spring weather took a turn back toward winter, he was sure he could ignore Uncle Sol's caution. Only when the unthinkable (in Rocky's mind) happened did he realize how right Uncle Sol was. It is always in the moments when the warned-of danger comes to pass that we realize how foolish we've been to take such chances.

In a similar manner, God seeks to spare us by giving us commandments to observe, not because God is a 'kill-joy' but because out of his great love for us, he wishes to keep us from suffering the grave consequences of our poor choices.

The fact that Rocky persuades and leads his friends into catastrophe only adds to his guilt. And Will ignored an important warning system inside himself in favor of looking good in the eyes of his older friends. There is plenty to explore in this story.

Questions

1. Have you ever ignored clear advice like Rocky and gotten into trouble because of it? Why are there rules for living? Why are there commandments from God?
2. Is it always easy to see the consequences of breaking rules right away like it was for Rocky and his friends? What if you break the rule of brushing your teeth after every meal? Will you see the consequence of that right away? Why might it be important to trust the rules given to you by experienced elders in your life?
3. Should Rocky have trusted Uncle Sol's advice? What makes someone's advice trustworthy? Why would you ignore the advice of someone you trust?
4. Is God's advice trustworthy? How do we know? Why would we ignore God's advice or break his commands if God is trustworthy?
5. Were Nick and Will guilty of going against Uncle Sol's advice since they didn't actually talk with Uncle Sol themselves? Will ignored a very clear warning in his head and heart that this action on the ice was dangerous. Would you have done what Will did or would you have just gone home? Seriously, now, if your friends were going to do something that you thought was too dangerous, but you really liked being with your friends and you wanted them to like you, would you go ahead even if your head was telling you stop?
6. What does it take to make a different choice from the crowd, especially if the 'crowd' is made up of your friends?
7. Does God expect us to make good choices that follow his commandments even when our 'crowd' is not making

good choices? How hard is that for you to do? How could you practice making choices that would make Jesus smile?
8. Uncle Sol has a hunch that the boys are making some bad choices. What if he had ignored the nudge he felt to do something? Have you ever felt a nudge from somewhere to help someone else or check on someone? Have you followed that nudge or ignored it? Can we ever know what might have happened if we followed the nudge that we ignored?
9. How might God use nudges to help people? Might God use you? Are you ready to listen? Are you ready to act? How do we figure out if a nudge is from God? Are there clues?

The Christmas Star

Matthew 2:1-11
Matthew 5:4

Christmas is the season of joy for Christians, but many people also experience a great sadness at Christmas time. In large part the sadness stems from memories of other Christmases when loved ones who are now gone were alive and vibrantly involved in their life. The loss of a beloved grandparent or neighbor or even a pet can be very traumatic for a child. Such a loss around Christmas time can have long lasting effects. Many adults carry the painful childhood memories of a profound loss that occurred around Christmas.

David had just such an experience. His beloved grandfather passed away quite unexpectedly right before Christmas. He feels the loss deeply and does the right thing by talking about it with his special neighbor, Uncle Sol. Uncle Sol just listens and lets the boy tell his story. It is a moment when David's budding faith is on the line. A quick dismissal of David's star story could easily crush the fragile hope onto which the boy is holding. Uncle Sol's own deep faith shows in his response to David. Children need to be around adults who have a strong faith foundation in order to feel the freedom to explore their own hopes and doubts in their growing relationship with God. Uncle Sol's affirmation allows his young neighbor to acknowledge the comforting presence of God and see it in the larger context of God's comforting message for all people for all time.

This story will allow you to explore issues of grieving, doubt, prayer, the role of the comforter, God's ways of communicating with us, the good news of Christmas and its relevance for us here and now.

Questions

1. David was very, very sad at the death of his grandfather. How could you tell that from the story?
2. Why do you think David ran from the farmhouse? Would you want to be with people or be alone when you are very, very sad? Why?
3. How did Uncle Sol help David?
4. When David saw the star, why do you suppose it calmed him down?
5. Why did David think that he was not actually praying? What do you think prayer is supposed to sound like? Where do you think you are supposed to pray? What does Uncle Sol say prayer actually is?
6. Why doesn't Uncle Sol laugh at David's question about thinking the star was a way for God to talk to David?
7. What was the connection that Uncle Sol made between David's experience with the star and God's message at Christmas?
8. Why do you think David wanted to celebrate Christmas after all?

Alligator Removal Services

Matthew 18: 15-35

Forgiveness is quite a challenging concept for adults, let alone children. Jesus is very clear about the critical nature of forgiveness in the life of a follower. In the Lord's Prayer Jesus teaches us to invite God to use our standards of forgiveness for others as the standard which God is to use on us (a proposition I find disconcerting to say the least!). In Jesus' parable of the Unmerciful Servant, we see clearly the dangers of choosing not to forgive. The chilling warning of Jesus at the conclusion of his little tale lets each disciple know the grave consequences of choosing not to forgive one another: "This is how my heavenly Father will treat each of you unless you forgive your brother or sister from your heart." The goal of this story is to communicate the necessity of forgiving so that we can live freely the life God intends for us.

Edie has hurt her best friend Alice by a thoughtless comment made in a moment of excitement following her selection as the lead in a school play. The subsequent nursing of that hurt by Alice builds a high barricade between the friends and no amount of effort on Edie's part allows her to get past Alice's defenses to renew the relationship; it is impossible. Alice quickly experiences the negative consequences of holding a grudge. The isolation and loneliness are very real. Uncle Sol's advice takes the form of sharing a story where two friends in a similar situation to Alice and Edie find a way to get past the offense in order to renew their friendship. First though, the wronged friend has to discover in a quite dramatic way the negative consequences of holding onto a grudge. The alligator represents the ugly, dangerous qualities of holding tightly to the resentment for wrongs experienced at the hand of another. The fact that the alligator grows every time the wrong is replayed in the mind is a way to convey how the lack of forgiveness makes the problem grow larger and larger over time. Only when the grudge-holder completely releases any claim to reparation for the wrong experienced can true freedom exist.

In many ways, young children are particularly adept at letting go of past offenses done to them. However, as they grow older, they learn that holding a grudge gives them a bit of power and that power is quite seductive ... at first. They do not realize the danger that awaits them in soul-crippling and life-snuffing ruminations that make their world become smaller and smaller as family and friends find them less and less pleasant to be with under any circumstances. Jesus wants to spare us from such a curtailed life both now and in the life to come. Try to help your students see the connections between this double story and God's desire for us to be free from anger and desires for revenge.

Questions

1. What happened between Alice and Edie? Why do you suppose Alice felt so hurt by Edie's comment? Do you think you might have felt the same way under similar conditions?
2. How did Alice decide to handle her hurt feelings? How did Edie decide to handle Alice's hurt feelings? What got in the way of the two girls becoming friendly with each other after the 'comment'?
3. How was the story that Uncle Sol read to Alice similar to Alice's experience?
4. What in the world was the alligator doing in the story? What does the alligator represent?
5. Why did the alligator keep growing? What did Grandfather know about the causes of alligator growth?
6. How did Angie and Tara rebuild their broken friendship?
7. How did the actions and words of Tara and Angie change when 'forgiveness' for the hurt they did to each other was offered? How might offering forgiveness for the hurt that Alice experienced change the ways Edie and Alice relate to each other?
8. Jesus said that we need to forgive. When Peter said to Jesus, "Master, how many times do I forgive a brother or sister who hurts me? Seven?" Jesus replied, "Seven! Hardly. Try seventy times seven." (Matthew 18: 21-22 Message). Do you think Jesus is exaggerating or telling us the

truth about the need to forgive others that much? Why do you think that? Can you follow Jesus' advice? Will you try?
9. Jesus also tells us that God wants us to forgive others like he forgives us. God's love is unconditional but his forgiveness is conditional according to Jesus. God will forgive us just as much as we forgive others. Does God keep a list of the things you do wrong every day or does he forgive you for your faults? Should you keep a list of the things people do wrong to you and remember everyone's bad treatment of you? What does Jesus say you should do? What will God do for you if you forgive people the wrong things they have done to you?

No Rushing Allowed

Jeremiah 29:4-11

Living in the moment, being present to the present is something children do quite naturally. When they are hungry, they want to eat; when they are tired, they want to sleep; when they need companionship, they seek out another with whom they can play. Emerging from the womb, children display utter impatience when a need is not met immediately. Tell a nursing baby to wait until the mother finds a suitable place to offer relief for those hunger pangs and the baby squalls its distress to the world. It is a sign of maturation for a child to be able to 'wait' for a need to be met. Optimistically we hope there is a corollary between the age of the child and an increasing length of time the child is able to 'wait' to have those needs met.

Unhappily, we are living in an age when our 'needs' and 'wants' have been purposefully blurred. Much energy is expended by advertisers to convince us that we 'need' certain items in order to thrive. The advertisers work very hard to transmute obvious 'wants' into 'needs'. Absolutely none of us is unaffected by this atmosphere. We have been breathing in this cultural air from the time we took our first breath. This atmosphere actually works to stunt our capacity to distinguish between the two and it has diminished our capacity to delay gratification of the real needs or the misappropriated wants.

In Jeremiah 29:4-11f, the exiles are expressly told to settle down and plan to stay for a very long while. The deep desire of the exiles to return home as quickly as possible is thwarted; still Jeremiah reassures them of God's timing and God's plan. It is not exactly what the exiles want to hear; at the very least the message is not giving them the time frame they want. While the promise of the return to their native land is welcome, the timing is not. The underlying reality is that God's timing is all that matters and that God is 'working his purpose out'. It is a challenging lesson to teach … that God's timing in and with our lives can be trusted. Will's hard-earned realization that grapes take a certain amount of time to ripen—that there is no shortcut to delicious sweet grapes—is a way children can begin to grasp the importance of this lesson.

Will's impatience with Uncle Sol's tending of the grapes as they near harvesting time is reflective of our own human impatience as we assess our lives and our current circumstances (personally, nationally or globally). We are confident, as is Will, that we can see what needs to be done and how to proceed if only someone, including God, would listen to us. Uncle Sol is patient with the young neighbor as he continues to hold the boundary firm since he alone knows how to achieve the desired outcome for his crop of grapes. Will tries to improve on Uncle Sol's method only to discover that it literally makes him sick. In the end, Will discovers that Uncle Sol really does know how to bring about the best result—sweet juicy grapes. And he is able to acknowledge that Uncle Sol not only knows what he was talking about, but that the best action Will can take is to trust his older neighbor and wait patiently as the process unfolds naturally. In Will's renewed desire to excel at waiting patiently for the hoped for outcome, there is a glimmer of evidence that he is taking an important step toward maturity.

Questions

1. What did Will do that would convince you that he did not trust what Uncle Sol said about ripening grapes?
2. How did Uncle Sol know that Will had been the one to 'thin' the bunches of grapes after he left him?
3. Why do you think Uncle Sol waited to speak with Will about taking care of his grapes while he was gone? Do you think that was a good idea?
4. Why might Will trust what Uncle Sol says about ripening fruit in the future?
5. Do you think Will might find it easier to trust what Uncle Sol says about other things in the future? Why or why not?
6. Why is it hard to wait for something you want?
7. What good things can you learn from waiting for something you want?
8. What can you do while you are waiting for something you want very badly?
9. How does God encourage us to wait for things he has promised us?
10. What kinds of things has God already provided in your life that would allow you to trust God's timing in other areas of your life?
11. If you take the passage from Jeremiah as a guide, how might you alter your prayers, your choices, your attitudes as you make your way through this life?

Neighborhood MVP

Luke 3: 21-22
Mark 1: 9-11
Matthew 3:13-17

Baptism is an outward and visible sign of an inward and spiritual grace. It is a mark of our acceptance into the corporate life of the Church—a sign and seal of our covenant with God. For those who practice infant baptism, the infant is ushered into the family of God through the covenantal promises of the parents and the community of faith itself. It is expected that (at an age when the community of faith determines children become accountable for their decisions) they will 'confirm' their parents' promises on their behalf and 'own' the covenant for themselves. For those who practice credo ("believer's") baptism, the moment of baptism is the birthing moment into a new life in Christ.

Growth in grace begins for all at baptism. Whether baptized as an infant or later in life through a profession of faith, when an individual becomes aware of the need for release from the debilitating reality of the human condition—sinners incapable of self-rescue—the only response is to turn to God for mercy and deliverance. We simply cannot make ourselves 'good', no matter how hard we try. We need help. Jesus Christ through his willing obedience through the suffering of the Cross provided humanity a pathway back to a reconciled relationship with the God-Who-Loves. The gift of the Holy Spirit, set loose by Christ to comfort his followers, confirms in each human heart the reality of the transforming change. Through baptism we " … received a spirit of adoption. When we cry, 'Abba! Father!' it is that very Spirit bearing witness with our spirit that we are children of God, and if children, then heirs, heirs of God and joint heirs with Christ—if, in fact, we suffer with him so that we may also be glorified with him." (Romans 8:15b-17)

Illuminating this core tenet of our faith for children is the point of Neighborhood MVP. Once again Rocky has done damage in Uncle Sol's garden. This time, there was no malice intent, only carelessness. Sadly the result is the same. Rocky does not hide from the responsibility for what he has done, but he is unable to repair the damage. Uncle Sol is deeply saddened by the loss, but his love for Rocky does not wane. When Uncle Sol becomes aware of Rocky's ripped team jacket which threatens the teen's standing with his coach, the elder neighbor provides a solution. He finds his son's jacket and gives it to Rocky to wear. Rocky is unwilling to accept his 'gift' because it carries the letters MVP on it. The teen feels completely unworthy to put the jacket on. Rocky's protest hinges on his being very unlike Uncle Sol's son. Uncle Sol doesn't view Rocky that way and ultimately convinces Rocky that when he looks at the teenager in the jacket, he 'sees' Rocky, but he also sees his son. Once Rocky is convinced that Uncle Sol is serious about the way he 'sees' his young neighbor, the teen is eager to become the young man Uncle Sol thinks he is.

Questions

1. Why isn't Uncle Sol mad at Rocky for ruining his trees?
2. What decision did Uncle Sol make a long time ago that determines how he looks at the children and teens in the neighborhood?
3. Does Rocky deserve Uncle Sol's help with the coach?
4. Why does Rocky have such a hard time accepting Uncle Sol's offer to loan him the MVP jacket?
5. Why doesn't Uncle Sol have a hard time loaning the jacket to Rocky?
6. How is Rocky like Adam, King David, Simon Peter, Saul of Tarsus?
7. How is Uncle Sol's response to Rocky's self-disparaging remarks similar to the ways Jesus responded to the outcasts of his own society?
8. How does God view those who have committed themselves to following Jesus Christ and publicly demonstrated this commitment through baptism?
9. Baptism symbolically represents death and rising to new life in Christ. In what ways is the symbol of the MVP jacket helpful in conveying a new life, a new person? What other symbols might you use to convey the inward spiritual grace that begins the process of becoming like Christ?

Some Birthday!

John 3:1-17

Playing with a puppet has limited appeal because once the novelty of moving the body parts and speaking for the puppet has worn off there are no surprises. It is usually fun for an audience to watch a puppet show because it is full of surprises and putting on a puppet show is fun because of the audience's response. But playing with a puppet by yourself loses the entertainment factor fast. Most people love happy surprises. Birthdays, recognitions, visits from friends and relatives one hasn't seen in a long time, winning a raffle all fall into the category of happy surprises. This story touches on the idea of trying to control people's actions and reactions towards us.

When Nicodemus met Jesus after dark to further his discussions about Jesus' message of the Kingdom of God, he heard Jesus refer to the Spirit blowing as the wind, showing up here … then there, bringing people into the realm of God just as God pleased, not as the gatekeepers of Jesus' day wanted. This was not a happy surprise for this respected and senior teacher. It was a disturbing message.

Throughout human history people have made every effort to control God and tend the gate, saying who could and could not be a part of the religious community. In ancient cultures sacrifices were offered to persuade the gods to do what the worshippers wanted. Although the ancient Hebrews were not instructed to think that God could be controlled, that did not keep them from imitating their neighbors who worshipped idols and practiced elaborate rituals to appease and persuade their gods.

Controlling God's movement is not possible. Jesus affirmed that the wind blows wherever it pleases. "You hear its sound, but you cannot tell where it comes from or where it is going. So it is with everyone born of the Spirit." What we can see is evidence of the Spirit's presence in people's lives. God brings into his family anyone and everyone who is willing to open his or her life to God, but the reality is, we cannot control God's coming and going.

God chose to do a new thing with and for humanity by sending Jesus to walk the earth with us. It was and it remains a great surprise for those who discover the truth of Jesus' words deep in their hearts. God's Spirit fills up willing souls wherever he finds them.

In the story, Nick is desperate to orchestrate his own birthday party. He is accustomed to birthday celebrations happening in certain ways around his house. When none of that seemed to be take shape on his special day he took matters into his own hands with disappointing results. Only when the surprise is sprung on him does Nick come to see that love and recognition cannot be controlled or manipulated or even predicted. Those who love and desire to give recognition will do so in their own way and in their own time. And it is all the sweeter because it is a surprise.

Questions

1. Why was Nick so disappointed? Why do we begin to expect things will never change when we've had a few experiences and celebrations that have been repeated in the same way? When can that be a good thing? When might that not be such a good thing?
2. Have you ever had a happy surprise? What was it? How did you react when you discovered the surprise? How might Nick have felt going from the lonely tree house party to the big gathering at Uncle Sol's house?
3. Jesus was trying to tell Nicodemus that God was not doing things the same old way. What images did he use to describe God's new work? Why might 'wind' be a good way to describe the way God moves in people's lives?
4. How is love both predictable and unpredictable? How was Nick's mother's love predictable and unpredictable? How was the love of Nick's friends both predictable and unpredictable?

The River Run

John 14:16-19, 25,26

How we understand the presence of the Holy Spirit in guiding us to all truth and bringing all things to our remembrance really will color how we live our day to day Christian lives. If we join disciples through the ages who have looked for the present reality of God in their daily choices and trials, then we are aware that there is a power that comes to us to do what we cannot accomplish by ourselves. If we do not look for God's Spirit to be with us through our days and nights, then the sad truth is we do not experience the very Presence that would make those days and nights much easier. Jesus told his disciples that they were already acquainted with the Holy Spirit—the Comforter—because it had been living with them and even in them.

In our own time, to speak of the working of the Holy Spirit in the lives of current faithful disciples is complicated. We are at a point in our history where people are not afraid to say they are "spiritual" or that they get "nudges" to do things. But many are not very clear about the source of their help. Jesus said, "I will ask the Father and he will give you another Counselor to be with you forever ... the Counselor, the Holy Spirit, whom the Father will send in my name, will teach you all things and will remind you of everything I have said to you." Christians have counted on that guidance since Pentecost. There are amazing stories that point to the active participation of God's Spirit in the lives of disciples here and now. Oddly, even among those who wear the name of Christ there are those for whom the Holy Spirit remains a mystery. Jesus said that the world cannot accept the Spirit of Truth because it neither sees him nor knows him. The Christ-followers who cannot see this Spirit of Truth have a greatly diminished experience of God's potent presence to help them in times of trouble.

While the story, The River Run, is not about the character of the Holy Spirit directly, it is meant to demonstrate the powerful truth that when the Holy Spirit dwells within a person it reminds that individual of the truths he or she has been taught already and gives the person new ways to put those truths to use . As Edie mulls over what Uncle Sol had said while the teens prepared for this summer adventure, she becomes very clear what his cryptic remark means. She is energized and becomes the catalyst for saving the group. From an outside perspective, it looks like Edie just "figured out" how to get off the river. But to Edie, it was as if Uncle Sol were right there giving her directions on what to do. That is the distinction. Jesus says that while the world cannot see or accept the activity of the Holy Spirit, the disciples know almost instinctively when he's present because they recognize him and the way he operates. That is why Edie wanted to immediately go and thank Uncle Sol for saving their lives. She knew where the knowledge had come from to help her and her friends extricate themselves from a very dangerous situation.

Conversations around the topic of the Holy Spirit would be particularly useful for older students.

Questions

1. Do you ever get "nudges" to do something good for someone? To help someone who is in trouble? Do you respond to those "nudges" or just ignore them?
2. How can you tell whether or not a "nudge" is from God's Spirit or from inside yourself?
3. Christ followers have always tested the "nudge" by asking if the "nudge" is in keeping with what Jesus would do and by exploring scripture to see if the "nudge" is in keeping with the Old and New Testaments, but particularly the New Testament. How might you explore "nudges" you get?
4. Have you heard or read stories about people who have followed the guidance of the Holy Spirit? The founding of the Plymouth Colony in America is one such story. Mother Teresa's founding of the Missionaries of Charity is another such story. Researching such stories can help

give shape to how we listen and watch for God's Spirit guiding us in the world here and now.

In fact, even as I finished writing this in a small public library, a little boy was waiting for his father to read the daily paper. He was bored; he was miserable; he moped. I felt a "nudge" to read to him. I kept writing about "nudges" and I felt the "nudge" again. So I put the writing down and asked the father if I could read a story to his son. The boy's face lit up. He hopped off the bench where he had been sitting and rushed to my side with exactly the book he wanted read to him. The father finished reading about the same time I finished the story. They thanked me and returned home. What will come of it? Who knows? That is for God to handle. But when Jesus said, "Whoever receives a child in my name receives me," he just might have meant, "Don't hesitate to read the boy a story."

Lilacs

Matthew 28:16-20
Acts 1:4-8

Love God, Love Others! The phrase is a shortcut way of referring to the Greatest Commandment: Love the Lord your God with all your heart, with all your soul, with all your mind. This is the first and greatest commandment. And the second is like it: 'Love your neighbor as yourself.' (Matthew 22:37-39) Dorotheus of Gaza, one of the desert fathers who lived during the 4th century, spoke of the way our relationship with God and others is like a wheel. We are spokes on that wheel and the closer we draw to the hub of the wheel (God), the closer we draw to one another and conversely, the farther we move away from each other, the farther we move away from God. Jesus' goal all along was to have the Good News of God's Reign spread throughout the world one by one by one. It began small, 11 followers who Jesus commissions to teach and to be heralds of this change in management. No longer are the old rules of the political world to hold sway. God's welcome, God's liberation, God's new rules for the world (on earth as it already is in heaven) are to be announced, embodied and spread to the ends of the earth.

Jesus' intention is for this message to be communicated by his eye-witnesses through words and in actions. The Book of Acts is exactly that … a recounting of the words and actions of his disciples as they follow his directive through the power of the Holy Spirit. Dorotheus was right. As we draw closer to one another in loving ways, we are, inevitably, in a better position to recognize God's real presence through the mystery of relationship.

Uncle Sol's neighborhood is all about relationships. His purpose has always been to help the children and teens around him learn to behave lovingly in relationships by modeling that himself, day in and day out. It is slow work. It is hidden work. The investment of time and energy may produce a beautiful bouquet of roses, but Uncle Sol can never be sure. He only knows that he is willing to spend his life trying to persuade others by his words and actions that there is a way to live that leads to abundant life. The story of the young soldier and the little "enemy" girl exchanging gifts is a backdrop for Rocky to 'understand' Uncle Sol. He knows by experience that love of neighbor has transformed his own life. Uncle Sol, who may have been the soldier or who may have been deeply moved by the words and actions of an older friend who served in World War II, was transformed himself. Since it has been Uncle Sol's goal to pass along his way of living to those about him, when he sees his son and Rocky relating to one another as he would, he witnesses two of his rose buds bursting into bloom. One by one the Good News of God's Reign is passed along, neighbor to neighbor stretching out to reach the ends of the earth.

Questions

1. Why do you think Rocky is so confident that Uncle Sol will care to see his prom pictures? What does it take for a person to believe another person cares about what he or she says or does?

2. Why do you think Rocky is so interested to find out why Uncle Sol is so kind, generous and loving toward people?
3. Can you tell by the way Hank relates to Rocky that he is very much like Uncle Sol himself? What clues do you take from the story?
4. How might the story about the soldier help Rocky grasp what is important to Uncle Sol? Does it matter whether the story is a true story about his neighbor's past? Why or why not?
5. What is the "evidence" Rocky points to after hearing the story that tells him the story is 'true' of Uncle Sol?
6. Jesus embodies God's Reign " … on earth as in heaven." By his words and by his deeds he announced that the Kingdom of God had come. He then hands on the responsibility to his disciples. Read Matthew 28:18-20, Luke 24:45-49, John 20:21-23. Though the accounts differ slightly, the central message is this: now the disciples are to be his witnesses. How does he assure the disciples that they will be able to do what he asks?
7. Uncle Sol is a faithful witness to the transforming effects of God's Reign in his own neighborhood. What did he see happening between Hank and Rocky that might encourage him?
8. How might you be a 'witness' for God's Reign on earth in your own life? What changes in behavior might you need to make in order for your life to be more reflective of God's way of doing things?
9. What might be better ways to relate to people in your life so that you are actually drawing closer to God like Dorotea suggested in the image of the wheel?
10. What does it mean to you to love God and love others? How might you start doing that more effectively? (Don't forget to ask for God's Holy Spirit to help you do so!)

Appendix C
Guide for Use of Cross-Over Stories that Work in Non-religious Settings

There are stories in this collection that have worked well in public school settings where I've been invited to tell stories. If teachers wish to explore character development through storytelling, I have selected stories that easily transfer to a non-religious setting and non-religious conversations. The questions are often open-ended enough to allow for a wide-ranging discussion of decision-making, responsibility, courage, kindness, and other related virtues that can help students succeed in life as cooperative and productive members of society.

A Drop of Faith

Trusting another human being with our lives is an important and often times frightening lesson for those unaccustomed to trusting others. Our current culture fosters excessive self-dependence. The words spoken by toddlers, "I can do it myself" have been elevated to a place of high regard in our day. The problem is—we can't do it ourselves. It's a lie. It's an illusion that breaks down when we stop and think more carefully about our lives: from relying on a electric grid to power our homes to counting on those who truck in foods from all around the globe into our local stores. We do little on our own that sustains our way of life. In reality we stand within an amazingly intricate web of trusting relationships with people we have never met. Our very health and well-being depend upon thousands and thousands of people doing their jobs correctly and well. The growing edge for children in the area of trust includes how to decide whom you can trust and how trust is reestablished once it has been lost.

In the story "A Drop of Faith," trust is the paramount issue. Can David trust Uncle Sol to actually catch him if he lets go of the branch? There are layers of trust in this narrative: trusting the laws of nature, trusting one's own strength, trusting a friend, trusting that promises made will be promises kept. Here are a few questions to prompt discussion with your students.

Questions

1. What makes you—as a listener—believe that Uncle Sol and David have a good relationship?
2. Does David cause Uncle Sol to wonder if he can continue to trust him in his yard?
3. Does Uncle Sol test David's willingness to trust him?
4. When Uncle Sol catches David, David has one more reason to trust Uncle Sol. What might have happened if Uncle Sol had dropped David? Would that be different than Uncle Sol catching David but then falling with David in his arms?
5. How does Uncle Sol set up the way David can prove he is trustworthy?
6. If David breaks his promise to Uncle Sol, how will that affect Uncle Sol's ability to trust David?
7. How do your students earn trust—yours, other students', administrators'? What are the ways students can regain a trust that has been broken? Between teacher and student? Between student and students?
8. What makes trust so important in a relationship?

Team Effort

"There is no 'I' in T E A M." It is a standard line used by every coach to try to get individual players to share the ball or to move play around the field or the court better. In a similar vein, John Donne wrote, "*No man is an island, entire of itself; every man is a piece of the continent, a part of the main; if a clod be washed away by the sea, Europe is the less … any man's death diminishes me, because I am involved in mankind.*" The sense of connection to all humanity and the recognition that each person contributes to the good of the whole community finds expression in these words.

Our cultural emphasis-to-excess on the individual's autonomy has led to much isolation and the lack of bonds between people in neighborhoods and whole communities. It seems the only time we discover the identity of our neighbors is during extreme conditions brought on by natural or humanly created disasters. After a catastrophic event people often comment, "The community came together. People were really there for each other." Once the trouble has passed, the sense of connection typically recedes into the background once again.

For a community to really thrive, individuals need to thrive. For individuals to thrive, they need to be recognized as valuable and contributing members to something greater than themselves. This story suggests that each person's contribution is unique and important for the benefit of the whole group. Kites and duct tape and safety pins are useful, in and of themselves, in very specific ways in very specific situations. However, when a new situation calls for it, something new and creative can happen with them. In like manner when individual strengths are pooled in a community or a classroom something greater and more creative can come into being. Encouraging students to look for the unique strengths in each other and to make a concerted effort to include everyone's gifts for the benefit of the whole group is a step away from isolating autonomy toward a unity that brings health and wholeness to all. Conversations around ideas of developing and encouraging community are critical for our young if they are to thrive as human beings.

Questions

1. In the story, Jenny lost something very valuable and needed help recovering it. When all the children began brainstorming solutions, some children's ideas were scoffed at as useless. How does criticizing ideas of one another cut off creativity?
2. How did Uncle Sol stop that tendency in the problem solving efforts?
3. What do you think went through Uncle Sol's mind when each neighbor brought his or her idea for solving the problem?
4. Uncle Sol managed to use all the contributions including Helen's hands. Later he helped the children discover the meaning of what they actually had done. Why do you think Uncle Sol worked so hard at helping the children see the point he was trying to make?
5. Are there people you ignore because you think they are 'useless'? What happens to you when you dismiss someone else as having no value? Think about how preconceived ideas of someone's value blinds us to seeing their genuine worth as a human being.
6. How have you felt and what did you do when people dismissed your ideas or your offer of help in a situation?
7. How might you help create a community—a sense of unity in your classroom? Your neighborhood?

Kite Calamity

In "The Kite Calamity", Julie learns several lessons. Chief among them is the importance of taking responsibility for her actions. A useful working definition of responsibility is making choices and accepting the consequences of those choices.

One of the important tasks of childhood, and parenting/teaching for that matter, is helping children become responsible for their own actions. Ultimately this sets the stage for becoming responsible adults who can contribute positively to society.

Questions

1. How does Julie show she is making steps in the right direction toward being a responsible person?
2. How does Uncle Sol show his confidence in her?
3. At what points does Julie demonstrate she is still learning about accepting the consequences of her choices?
4. How do Julie's parents help her learn about living with the consequences of her choices?
5. Do you think holding Julie accountable for the payment of this bill from the electric company is a good way to teach this lesson? If so explain why. If not, explain why not and what other ways one might teach the important lesson of accepting the consequences of one's choices.
6. Is Uncle Sol's intervention—with Julie's parents' permission—a good idea? Would it help or hurt Julie learning the lesson? How so?
7. In what ways do your students learn to be responsible? Encourage conversation about ways students learn to be accountable for their choices at home, at school, on teams, etc.
    a. What makes it hard for students to accept the consequences of their choices?
    b. How does the prevailing culture at school, home and in the community at large encourage or discourage taking responsibility for one's actions?

Lemonade Wisdom

Understanding instruction, learning new skills, acquiring new knowledge is not simply a matter of a teacher imparting facts and figures to an untouched blank slate. Young minds are in various stages of formation. Sometimes those young minds are full of inaccurate information or skills learned incorrectly, or erroneous knowledge which has to be replaced. Sometimes the information is accurate, but the student is so impressed with it that he or she isn't very open to additional information a teacher can impart. In such situations, pointing out the student's obviously inadequate foundation often entrenches the student in his or her position. Arguing with a close-minded student gets the instructor nowhere, but there are ways to create receptivity. Uncle Sol has a unique way of helping a young neighbor see how closed her mind actually is to new information.

Because this story is based on a teaching from ancient wisdom traditions in Egypt and intended for adult learners, there is an application for the teacher of older students. Helping the older student see the value of keeping an open mind is often a challenge. Some believe holding firmly to their particular position or their way of seeing is a sign of their strength. Depending on the subject, that might be true. Exploring the difference between strongly held convictions worth standing up for versus rigidly held ideas based on misinformation would be a worthwhile conversation to have with middle school and high school students. Guiding the conversation about Uncle Sol's lesson with the lemonade for younger children could begin with these kinds of questions.

Questions

1. What did Edie say she wanted from Uncle Sol? Did she really want it? How can you tell?
2. What was your first clue that Uncle Sol was a bit frustrated with Edie's constant interruptions?
3. What did you think when you first heard that Uncle Sol kept pouring the lemonade so that it spilled everywhere?
4. Do you think that Uncle Sol's method of teaching a lesson is effective? Would it work on you?

5. Do you sometimes think you know so much about a subject that you don't need to listen to what anyone else has to say about the subject? How do people react to you if you do that?
6. How can you keep from shutting the door to your brain in times like that?

For older students additional questions might include:

1. What is the difference between an open and a closed mind? Is an open mind always a good thing? Is a closed mind always a bad thing? Can you think of illustrations where an open mind is a bad thing and a closed mind is a good thing?
2. How should you treat someone with a closed mind about things you think are important? Is that the way Uncle Sol treated Edie?
3. Was Uncle Sol's way of teaching Edie respectful or disrespectful of Edie?
4. How can you tell when it might be important to keep an open mind? A closed mind?

An Unexpected Flower

Life is hard. We try to protect ourselves and our children from the 'hardness' but like Sleeping Beauty's parents, who unsuccessfully attempted to remove every possible spindle from their kingdom to keep their daughter safe, we fail. Bad things happen to good and bad people alike. Human responses to the hard, bad things can be just as hurtful and damaging. If one has experienced deep hurt like Rocky and follows it by hurting another person as Rocky did in vandalizing Uncle Sol's garden, a downward spiral begins unless something intervenes to stop it.

Uncle Sol does not live in the world of retribution and retaliation. He wants to invite something different to emerge from people who make mistakes—even serious mistakes. In many ways Uncle Sol could belong to a group of people who advocate radical gracefulness in human relationships. He is quick to forgive even when all of his neighbors think he should not. He understands that he has experienced a lot of forgiveness in his own life. That forgiveness has freed him to get on with his life and put mistakes behind him, learn new ways of relating to people he loves and the world at large. He wants to offer that opportunity to individuals who in some way have harmed him.

Because Uncle Sol knows Rocky's story, he is more than willing to give Rocky a second chance. Because Uncle Sol understands human nature, he is willing to give all his neighbors second, third and fourth chances to improve the way they relate to him and to one another. Imagine a world where people said, "I'm sorry" and meant it; a world where the injured party said, "I forgive you" and meant it, too. Perhaps that world can begin in your classroom. Encourage your students to think about being radically graceful with each other. Help them to understand the importance of forgiveness in making the world inside themselves right as well as the world beyond themselves. Look at Appendix C for Alligator Removal Services for more on the importance of forgiveness.

Questions

1. What do flowers need to grow well?
2. What do people need to grow well?
3. What is the significance of the title, *An Unexpected Flower*?
4. How is Uncle Sol not only a good gardener of flowers, but a good gardener of people?
5. Should Rocky be given a second chance? Have you ever needed a second chance? How does it feel when someone gives you another chance to prove you have learned your lesson?
6. Why is it important to give someone who is really sorry for what they have done a second chance? What might happen if they are not given a chance to prove they have changed?

APPENDIX C / 243

7. Do you think Uncle Sol will hold Rocky's terrible mistake against him even if he gives him a second chance? Do you think Rocky will hold it against himself? Do you think Rocky will be able to believe that Uncle Sol really is giving a chance at a new beginning to him and the rest of the kids in the neighborhood? What will it take for Rocky to believe it?
8. How can you help people you forgive know that you mean it?

Trusting the Clues

How knowledge is passed from one generation to another has been the source of serious study for millennia. What is the nature of knowledge that it can be passed along anyway? What is "knowing" in the first place? Such questions fascinate philosophers and drive the philosophically challenged fleeing for the door. However, it is important to think about the best ways for information and for knowledge to be passed along. We are in the transition time between print as the repository of our knowledge and back-up drives that keep our information well-organized. Our children still use books even as they learn the use of operating systems on their computers. We do not know where the future will take us in regards to keeping our collective knowledge. We have already discovered that floppy discs and hard discs that were used in conjunction with ancient computers cannot be read unless one has access to ancient machines or computer operators with special translation equipment. In that regard, books are 'safer' and more reliable since they cannot lose their operating system. They have a longevity as yet unmatched by machines that need power to operate.

Even more valuable than a book is the repository of knowledge found in the mind, heart and hands of a living person. A child can read a book or go on-line to watch how to throw a lump of clay onto a wheel to form a pot. Or a child can watch a real, live potter throw clay onto the spinning wheel, observe the effect of the water that is added and see the movement of the hands as the clay pitcher takes shape. That same child may have the good fortune to have the potter step back and invite the child to give it a try, guiding her young hands in molding the pitcher herself. The handing on of tradition, knowledge and skill that can be done from adult to child in a one-on-one relationship is an age-old system of preserving accumulated human knowledge. In the medieval period it was called 'apprenticeship'. It worked well. There are important ways we learn by watching a real live person doing the actual skill we are trying to learn. The popularity of the cooking shows attest to that, but how much more effective, if we are whipping up our first cheesecake, to have a cheesecake expert by our side guiding us.

In this story, Will becomes the clue, the guide, the passer-on of knowledge. He is able to guide the treasure seekers to their destination, but first they have to recognize that he is the clue. This story is a disguised plea for more humane, mentoring relationships between old and young in an age where technology builds a wireless wall between generations. People embody knowledge. They carry it, they can share it, and they can confirm that the knowledge has been rightly received by watching/listening to the learner. It is a beautiful loop system. Discover how many mentoring relationships your students have or have had in their young lives so far.

Questions

1. Who taught you to tie your shoes? How did you learn to throw a ball?
2. Can you learn to whistle by reading a book?
3. Is it possible to use a computer to learn how to paint a picture well?
4. Why is it easier to learn something if a person shows you and stays with you while you are learning and practicing?
5. How was Will able to guide the other treasure seekers to the hidden tree house? Will the treasure seekers be able to

guide others to the tree house? Where is the knowledge of how to get there located?
6. Do you have any mentors? Explain what that means. Grandparents, parents, teachers, coaches are all examples of mentors for certain kinds of knowledge.
7. Are you are mentor to someone? Explore how students can use the knowledge they have already acquired to help children younger than themselves acquire the same skills.

Seeing the Truth

Seeing beneath the surface has been a point of emphasis for years among educators who truly want to help each student excel. The more agencies and institutions try to lump children together in order to measure their skill progress, the more some of us push back from them to recognize the uniqueness of each learner. The same is true in the realm of advertising. The advertising industry thrives on teaching consumers to only count the externals that can be altered with clothing or make-up or work-out machines and the like. The thoughtful ones among us consistently shoot back saying, "No, appearance is not the measure of the worth of a person."

A person's worth is not based on looks or brains or wealth. In America there is a basic core belief that each individual counts. We falter in the living out of that ideal, but it is nonetheless foundational for us as a nation. Looking past the externals is what this story is about. Uncle Sol sees something deeper—a deeper truth about people and in this particular case, a deeper truth about the animal. For children who are real animal lovers or who have had a pet hit by a car or have recently lost a dear pet, this story could be a bit difficult to hear. Nevertheless, this story could, in fact, really give your students an opportunity to discuss the loss of a beloved pet or relative and the impact of that in their lives. You might not begin a conversation here or with that outcome in mind yet still find your students will take you there anyway. As always, use your judgment as to the usefulness of this tale in your classroom.

Questions

1. What part of the story did you like the most? Why?
2. Was there any part of the story that made you sad?
3. On the way home from the veterinarian when Nick was so sad, do you think Uncle Sol was just trying to make him feel better when he said he thought Kristy might make it through the night?
4. What do you think about Uncle Sol's comment that he could see the heart of a person or in this case the heart of Kristy? Since he did not mean a real heart, what did Uncle Sol actually mean?
5. What do adults mean when they say "That kid shows such heart." or "That team played with so much heart"? What are they seeing in the person that makes them say that?
6. What can the kinds of clothing a person wears tell you about a person?
7. Can a person be very smart and wear ragged clothes? Can a person be very dumb and wear beautiful clothes? Can a person be smart and wear very nice clothes? Or dumb and wear ragged clothes? What do the clothes actually tell you about a person?
8. How can we tell about the heart of a person? What did Uncle Sol say he uses to measure the heart of a person? Can that work for you?
9. What good things can come of looking past the surface to the deeper part of your classmates? Your friends? People on the street?
10. What is challenging about learning to look deeper?

The Sliding Hill

"Choose me!" "Choose me!" The cry has been heard across playgrounds for generations as teams are formed for kickball and all other sorts of games. The elation felt by the child who is chosen first or at least early is in direct contrast to the child who waits as the pool of choices gets smaller and smaller, signaling to everyone that the remaining children are undesirable as teammates. Experiencing the joy of being chosen marks a person inwardly. Whether a child is set apart from his or her peers because of athletic skill or superior knowledge or leadership qualities, the effect on the growing spirit in that child is noticeable. We see a 'chosen' child demonstrate more confidence, more drive, more leadership. That is all to the good and to be lauded. However, because children have much maturing to do in their understanding of themselves and their peers, we also see 'chosen' children get carried away with their special position. Too often children who are 'chosen' see their status as a way to exercise privilege. In short, they take advantage of their position on a team or in a classroom. Mostly this is not shown in the presence of adults, but saved for the unsupervised moments when privilege can be asserted over less powerful peers.

This is precisely what happens in the story of "The Sliding Hill". Edie is chosen as a 'protector' for the younger children in the neighborhood. She does her job well until there is a time when she herself is unsupervised and then she takes advantage of the privilege. Edie is guided by Uncle Sol into the proper understanding of her role as his chosen 'protector'.

Questions

1. What was the job Edie was chosen to do?
2. Why would Uncle Sol choose one of the older neighborhood children to be a 'protector'? Do you think that was a good idea?

3. Do you think Edie felt special because Uncle Sol had chosen her to do the job of 'protector'?
4. Did Edie's being chosen for the job of 'protector' mean she had more time to play on the sliding hill herself or less?
5. Is it always true when you are chosen to be the leader that there is more responsibility and less time for 'fun'?
6. If Edie was tired of the job Uncle Sol had given her, what could she have done?
7. How did Edie abuse her role as 'protector' of the little children?
8. Are leaders supposed to look out for themselves first? Why or why not?
9. How did Edie learn that she misused her position? Was Uncle Sol's way of correcting Edie a good way? Why? Or why not?
10. What lessons do you think Edie learned here?
11. What lessons might you take away from this story and this conversation?

Lessons in Freezing

"No running in the halls!" "Line up here on the yellow line." "Don't push the person ahead of you." A school functions on rules of behavior. Homes operate with rules, as well, though learned more through verbal instruction and modeling then with a written code. There are also the laws of nature which impact all living beings, like ice melting when the temperature is above freezing. Rules, regulations, and laws all have an air of restriction about them. For any community to function well, rules need to be established and followed. The Rule of Law is critical for a democratic society to maintain order. Learning to obey rules and disciplining oneself to be one's own inner "police officer" is an integral and critical part of maturation paving the way for satisfying, mutually respectful adult relationships.

People have a funny relationship with rules. Often, they want rules applied to other people fairly, but firmly while at the same time they want the rules to be relaxed when applied to their own circumstances. Artists of various stripes, celebrities in any field and some business people seem to know how to "skirt" the rules and get away with it. Many people even applaud such rule-bending or breaking—a kind of underground "cult" that supports resisting authority. Yet most people know that 'the rules don't apply to me' behavior is not only unfair, but wrong and undermines us all.

In order to teach children the impact of following rules or laws, it is critical to have a fair and equitable way of administering consequences for rule-breaking. There needs to be a consistent enforcement of the consequences in order for children/students to internalize the reasons for restraining themselves. Now there are situations where the circumstances themselves teach better than any engineered set of consequences. When Rocky chooses to ignore the counsel of Uncle Sol regarding the safety of the ice, unbeknownst to him, he is on course to learn a very important physics lesson. He is also about to learn the value of following rules even when they seem to come from overly-cautious adults giving "kill-joy" advice.

Rules and laws are in place for the protection of individuals and for the protection and survival of the community. Helping children consciously grasp the positive aspects of rules is a great service to them and to the communities in which they live. Conversations about the rationale behind the limits you have set in the classroom, the rules at school, the rules at home and in the community, about natural laws that impact their very existence can all be very helpful. Perhaps the story of Rocky, Nick and Will ignoring the laws of nature and Uncle Sol's advice about those very laws will help you jump-start such an exchange with your students.

Questions

1. Why would Rocky ignore Uncle Sol's advice? How does our personal desire to do something often contribute to the breaking of rules/laws? Do you think Rocky and his friends will ever go out on old ice again? Why or why not?
2. Do you find it easy or difficult to follow rules? Why?
3. Do you think if a rule is unfair in your mind it is okay to ignore it? Why? Why not?
4. Do you enjoy being around other people who break the rules like cutting in line ahead of you? Cheating on homework? Taking more than they are supposed to when snacks are handed out? Why does that bother you? If you are the one doing the rule breaking, can you understand why people get upset with you?
5. How is the development of trusting relationships related to keeping rules? How might trust in relationships be hurt by people who always break the rules?
6. Do you think Uncle Sol will trust Rocky to follow his advice from now on? Why? Why not?

Alligator Removal Services

Forgiveness is a quality that has received much press lately. A quick survey online gives a multitude of studies, both secular and religious, that point to the mental health benefits of forgiveness. For people to be healthy, developing the capacity to forgive is actually a form of self-care. It is not a natural response to being wronged. Consequently, the exploration of the idea of forgiveness along with potential methods of forgiving is important in order to give children a basis for choosing forgiveness as a response to wrongs.

In this story, the two best friends have a falling out because of a comment made by one after school. The reaction of the hurt friend is a natural one. Alice resents Edie and so she breaks off all friendship ties. The ensuing isolation and loneliness are also typical experiences of those who hold grudges against former good friends. When Alice feels the grudge taking over her life, she turns to Uncle Sol for advice. Uncle Sol finds a way to help Alice see her problem for what it is: a growing menace that takes all the fun out of life.

The story within the story tells of two girls who once were best friends until one girl said an unintentional, unkind thing to the other. The hurt girl, Angie, finds a "rock" to carry around to remind her of the offensive remark made by Tara. The rock is not a rock and hatches into an alligator that grows with each rehearsal of the "terrible moment" between the two former friends. Angie learns the secret of how to get rid of the alligator once she realizes that it is ruining her life. This, in turn, helps Alice figure out how to open up the lines of communication with her former best friend so that her own life will not continue to be so negatively influenced by the bad interaction she had with Edie.

Questions

1. Have you ever had someone say something that hurt your feelings? What did you do about it?
2. Is it easy or hard to act like Alice and like Angie when a friend hurts your feelings? Why?
3. What happened to Alice and to Angie that made them want things to be back to normal with their friends?
4. How are grudges/resentments like the alligator in the story? Is it easy or hard to be around someone who is resentful and angry? Why?
5. Is it easy for a person to live with themselves when they are resentful and angry? What makes it so hard?
6. Does Grandfather's advice make sense to you? Why or why not?
7. Why is it so hard to get rid of the alligator in the story? Why is it so hard to get rid of resentful feelings?
8. What finally made the alligator disappear? What can finally make our resentments go away?

9. How might you practice forgiving people who have hurt your feelings? Is there anyone in your life you could forgive right now?

One important comment to make about forgiveness is that it is not the equivalent of being a perennial victim. Sometimes children (and adults) are actually experiencing abuse at the hands of another. Forgiveness in such circumstances is still critical, but it does not mean ignoring or allowing the abuse. It is important to know that forgiveness does not equal having no voice or strength to resist abusive situations, but once the abuse has been stopped, forgiveness in such circumstances is still critical for one's own mental and spiritual health. Forgiveness does not require us to forget that some people are just plain dangerous for us to be with. Making a wide path around them even after we have forgiven them is perfectly permissible.

No Rushing Allowed

There is not a child in our society who doesn't say, "I wish 'x' would hurry up and happen." It is a mark of young childhood to be impatient when what is wanted is not quickly forthcoming. Conversely it is a sign of growing maturity when a child is able to delay gratification for a better outcome. Helping children appreciate the importance of delaying gratification is an admirable goal which is thwarted on every side by our current cultural emphasis on obtaining 'what you want, when you want it, the way you want it.'

The task of education is an exercise in delayed gratification. Learning to spell seems a long way from writing that crucial letter of introduction to a potential employer. The slow work of learning how to add and subtract, multiply and divide properly seems light years away from using sophisticated calculators to determine the slope of a roof on the new building. Gathering the building blocks for mature thinking always takes time and there are always young learners who are impatient with the process. Why not just use the calculator

APPENDIX C / 253

and skip learning the math behind it which guides it's functioning in the first place? The dangers of short-circuiting the necessary preparation are not always easy to grasp. The value of delaying gratification is hard to grasp, as well. When the pay-off may not be experienced until a generation or two in the future, it is even more difficult to convince students or their parents that sacrifices now are critical for quality of life to be present for generations yet unborn.

"No Rushing Allowed", may allow you to begin a conversation on the value of delayed gratification with your students.

Questions

1. What is the most important point in this story about Will and the grapes?
2. What other lessons do you think Will learned about grapes? About himself?
3. Did you think Uncle Sol's way of teaching Will about the importance of waiting was helpful? Why or why not?
4. Who has taught you about waiting? How well have you learned the lesson he or she is trying to teach you?
5. Do you think being patient is easy or difficult? Are there certain people with whom you could try to be more patient? How about circumstances where you know patience would be a good idea?
6. What good might come from waiting patiently for something to come to pass? What if it is waiting for your birthday party? What if it is waiting for your driver's license?
7. Can waiting impatiently ruin the very thing you are waiting for? Can you think of any examples?
8. What do you think grown-ups have to wait for? Do you think that is hard for them? Would they tell you it is important to wait patiently?
9. What are you looking forward to doing as an adult? Can you wait patiently for that privilege? Would there be anything useful about being impatient as you wait for some-

thing to happen when you are an adult? What might that be?
10. Name some things really important to you in your life about which you can practice being patient.

"Neighborhood MVP"

In the story, Neighborhood MVP, there are a number of important teaching points that can be explored. Rocky continues to live in the moment without thinking about potential consequences to his actions. Playing laser tag, with escape from his pursuer foremost in his mind, he completely loses track of where he is and what he must avoid in Uncle Sol's yard. The consequences are dire for the young apple trees and Rocky fears the consequences will be dire for his relationship with Uncle Sol. One very important difference in Rocky's reaction to his blunder in the garden this time (see "The Unexpected Flower") is his acceptance of responsibility for what happened. He tells Uncle Sol that he has ruined the trees. Uncle Sol's reaction is both expected and unexpected. He is very disappointed about the trees, but he is not disappointed with Rocky. He doesn't yell. He doesn't banish Rocky from the backyard. He accepts Rocky's remorse. It is clear from Uncle Sol's reaction that he sees the tree destruction as an accident and Rocky is forgiven.

In a very real, but unstated manner, Uncle Sol has chosen consciously to be a mentor to the children in the neighborhood through his actions and his words. He genuinely welcomes the young neighbors into his yard and into his heart. He chooses to treat all of them with the kind of love and regard one usually reserves for family alone. Uncle Sol just expands his understanding of who is included in his family. Rocky has a hard time believing that this adult truly cares about his well-being, though he can acknowledge that his elder neighbor does show deep care for all the other children and teens in the neighborhood. Rocky's resolve to be like

Hank (Uncle Sol's son) is his response to the unconditional love he experiences.

Rocky's father had died of cancer when he was just beginning to enter adolescence (see The Unexpected Flower). His sorrow, confusion and rage had crippled his normal development. He was a boy at risk ... until he met Uncle Sol. Resilient kids, those who make it despite having had an especially difficult time negotiating childhood due to abuse, trauma or extreme stress, usually are resilient because there is one adult in their lives who takes a great interest in them. The healing of those young wounded spirits comes from the wonder-filled belief that one mature person cares deeply about them and their success in life. Such a significant person can be a grandparent, an aunt, an uncle, a coach, a member of the clergy, a teacher, a neighbor, an employer, some adult who helps the at-risk child or youth believe in him or herself. Such a person has truly become the mentor-master ('master' in the sense of the old medieval guilds) and the youth has become the apprentice. The relationship is never spoken of in these terms, but the willingness of the mentor-master to share knowledge gained through life experiences and the willingness of the apprentice to incorporate these 'lessons' into living reality in their own life is what makes the bond between the two work its miracle of repair and restoration

Sadly, there are many students who do not experience this kind of genuine welcome in the lives of adults. Perhaps through story, they too can begin to know the qualities that exist in adults who can be trusted to lead them into maturity with grace.

Questions

1. How could Rocky have avoided knocking down the apple trees?
2. What reaction would you expect from Uncle Sol? Why?
3. What is surprising about Uncle Sol's offer to loan Rocky his son's jacket?

4. Why do you think Rocky finally accepts Uncle Sol's offer? What does it take for you to believe someone genuinely means what they say?
5. Rocky accepts responsibility for his actions. What difference does it make the reaction of the person we have wronged when we accept responsibility for our actions?
6. What relationship skills does Uncle Sol as a mentor-master demonstrate to Rocky and to the others in the neighborhood?
7. How does Rocky show that he understands the lessons Uncle Sol teaches him about relating to others?
8. How might Rocky behave differently now that he is wearing Hank's jacket? Do you think the changes in his behavior will only be on the basketball court? Do you think Rocky will show changes in his behavior toward others off the court? Why?
9. Do you behave differently when you know someone trusts you, believes in you, sees the best in you? Why?
10. Is it possible for a fellow student to help another student believe in themselves? How well do you think such efforts to help another would be received?
11. Some define unconditional love as "unconquerable good will" toward another person. Is this a possible standard for students to choose? For adults? What might the world look like if kids and adults chose to be like Uncle Sol?

Some Birthday

The birth of a child is a momentous occasion in the life of a family, an event that can bring pure joy, mixed feelings, or outright distress. Some children hearing this story may have been desperately wanted, while others may sense or believe they created hardships by their arrival. Some may have been adopted and may or may not realize that the most loving thing their birth parents could do for them was to make it possible for them to become part of a family that could fully love and care for them. The varied experiences children have had around the celebrations of their birthdays may set the stage for this story to raise a number of challenging emotions for some children. Although it varies from family to family, our culture has some pretty clear guidelines about how to celebrate a birthday, generally including at least singing the "Happy Birthday Song", having a cake and receiving some gifts from the family and a few close friends.

Even if children have never had a birthday celebration at home that matches the party that Nick experiences, they can understand the shock and disbelief when no one, including his own mother, seems to care that it is his birthday. At the same time, there may be children who have had the 'being forgotten' part of the experience without the happy outcome. It would be important to be prepared for comments about such experiences in any discussion you might have about the contents of this story.

Nick discovered that he really did have a mother, father and friends who cared about him, but he also discovered that he was not in charge of how they expressed their love for him. He attempted to make his own party with dismal results. Expressions of love can not be forced or manipulated by the person seeking to be treasured. Resentment among children grows very quickly when the 'bossy' one tells each child how to act towards her or him, "You need to come to my house at 2:00 p.m. and you need to wear a nice dress and then you have to be nice to me and share whatever I tell you to share." Not many children will find such direct demands very inviting. If a child grows up being allowed to demand attention and force 'treasuring' behavior, he or she will have a very rude awakening as she moves into adolescence and adulthood. Fortunately Nick is not practiced at demanding love and attention. He is just sorely disappointed that no one seems to care.

Uncle Sol is in on the surprise for Nick and helps make the birthday celebration even better than Nick could have planned for himself. Conversations after this story could center on how one handles disappointment, ways of showing friends we care about them, handling surprises both pleasant and unpleasant, and trying to force friendship.

Questions

1. Why did Nick's feelings get so hurt?
2. What might you assume about the birthday celebrations that Nick is used to having at his house from the way he got so disappointed?
3. How did he handle his disappointment? How do you handle situations that disappoint you?
4. How are birthdays celebrated in your home? Do you know how birthdays are celebrated in other countries? You might look up birthday traditions in other lands.
5. Nick really got a surprise when he went into Uncle Sol's home. There are happy surprises and there are unhappy surprises. What are some of the happy surprises you have experienced? How did you react to a happy surprise? How did you react to an unhappy surprise? (Making a foray into the unhappy surprises may bring up far more information from your students' lives than is appropriate in a classroom setting; as usual, use your judgment here.)
6. Do you think Nick's family and friends had a good time planning the surprise party for Nick? Do you think any of them anticipated how disappointed and unhappy Nick would be while thinking nobody cared about him? What might his friends have done that could have made Nick feel okay without giving away the surprise?
7. Nick tried to make his own party by inviting all his friends to his own special party that he was going to do all by himself since his mother had forgotten. Clearly it didn't work. What clues did Nick get that let him know planning his own birthday party just wasn't a good idea? Have you ever tried to make something happen that just wasn't working right? Did you pay attention to the clues that let you know you were just going against the expected order of things? What happens to people who ig-

nore clues that they are doing something that isn't going to work? How can you learn to pay attention to the clues life gives you about heading in the right or the wrong direction?

The River Run

Preparing for an adventure must take place on many levels. There is the physical aspect of preparation, getting the supplies and equipment one needs for the adventure itself. Then there is the knowledge preparation that must take place, understanding what the particular challenges are going to be and the best ways to overcome those challenges. Another area of preparation that people seldom talk about is the 'what if' part of preparation: imagining something going wrong and figuring out how one might best respond in the moment if that should happen. It is very good mental practice to imagine various scenarios that would require quick action. Though chances are good the adventurer will never have to call on that specific knowledge, just having practiced thinking quickly is helpful.

The four teens thought they were ready for their adventure. Some of them had already had an outing on the river which convinced them that they knew what to expect the day of the river trip. The group had done some of its homework: they had the necessary gear they needed for the trip; they had talked extensively with each other and with Uncle Sol so they felt they had "researched" the river. What they had neglected to do was think through some "what ifs". Fortunately, Uncle Sol gave the group a bit of cryptic advice which ended up being the most helpful piece when they got into their predicament.

Edie ultimately had to go beyond what she knew from her river research and pay attention to advice that Uncle Sol had given. As she bounced against the log, she could let her mind wander and allow her imagination to work for her. It was so important that she knew both her abilities and her liabilities which ultimately let her trust her intuition to follow Uncle Sol's puzzling advice despite the protest of the boys.

Learning to trust one's inner guidance system is a delicate and life-long learning project that begins in childhood. Our minds are able to pull together far more information than we consciously process. In the twinkling of an eye Edie was able to put together many pieces of what needed to happen if she was to save herself and her friends, beginning with breaking the cardinal rule and getting off the tube. She knew intuitively that she had the skill to balance on the tube and jump onto the log, and Uncle Sol had given her permission to trust her intuition.

Practicing trusting one's intuition is important. It can be life-saving. Additionally, this story can prompt all kinds of conversations with your students: rites of passage for teens in your area that children look forward to, taking good risks versus bad risks, trusting your intuition or inner voice, expressing gratitude to people who help you by being on the scene or through a remembered conversation like the one Edie had had with Uncle Sol.

Questions

1. In Uncle Sol's neighborhood one sign of being a teenager was being allowed to make a run down the river. Are there any "signs" in your community that signal the crossover from being a child to a teen? Is it a good idea to have a 'rite of passage'? It might be useful to talk with students about rites of passage in more primitive cultures and compare and contrast that with our own.
2. There are "good risks", real challenges that have a 'scare factor' in them but which still are essentially controlled risks. These help teens test their courage and develop self-confidence. The run down the river was a challenge of this sort, even though at times the risk really was quite high. Other risks are "bad risks," giving thrills to the risk-takers because the 'scare factor' is real in the form of get-

ting caught by the police for stealing or drinking or using dope of some sort. Learning to take 'good risks' that are full of moderate danger and excitement is an important way to grow while avoiding the terrible consequences of thrill seeking in negative ways. What do you think makes a risk one worth taking? Why?

3. Learning to trust one's inner guidance system is a much harder lesson, but it is actually something you practice every day. You watch your teacher come in the door and you take a reading of your teacher's mood. You may never say it out loud, but some of you will immediately pick up on the way your teacher puts down her book bag, whether he carefully places his coat over the chair or throws it down. All the clues your teacher gives off are scanned and interpreted by you without even really thinking about it. Some of you are scanning your environment all the time and you use that gathered information to make decisions. Most of the time the information gathering goes on unconsciously and you are unaware of how much data you have gathered and how often you use it. How did Edie know what to do? No one told her to get off her tube; no one told her to use the skills she had gained playing on the lake; no one told her she actually could do what she imagined. Why did she do it? When have you trusted yourself in a similar situation? How did you know what to do? Explore different ways of 'knowing' and 'gathering' information.

Lilacs

What constitutes a good person? A good member of society? A good citizen? And how do you cultivate those qualities and virtues after you have identified them? Every culture seeks to enumerate the qualities that it wants to teach its young in order for the cultural values to be transmitted to future generations. You are engaged in just such an enterprise at this very moment. You are seeking to mold the young in your care with ideas ... ideas about how human interactions should work between people and across generations. This is no small task! It is most certainly not the province of societal entrepreneurs who recommend doing "something new and creative" (though many seek to promote just such an attitude.)

To teach the young the virtues that transmit across generations, it is important to not only have a clear idea of what those virtues are ... it is important to make valiant efforts to embody them. Virtues are not taught so much as they are "caught." The Nobel Prize Winner for Peace in 1979, Mother Teresa, modeled one very effective way to make a difference in the world. She once said, "We cannot do great things, but we can do small things with great love." Such an attitude in fact did accomplish great things. The small things matter. The 'thank you' spoken, the door held open, the smile that welcomes conversations, the quick willingness to help when one sees another in trouble, the generous offering to share what one has with another are all 'small things' that make all the difference in the quality of life in a society.

One such movement to energize people toward good, kind, generous actions toward others currently in fashion is known as 'Pay It Forward'. It takes its name from a book and film by that same title. The concept is simple: instead of paying someone 'back' as one feels obligated to do by all our social training ... instead of that ... you pay it 'forward' to someone else. When you have been given a helping hand, you in turn give a helping hand to another. If someone has eased your burden, made your life a bit easier, you look for opportunities to do the same for a different person who crosses your path who may be in similar straits.

When we experience the kindness and generosity of another person, it is possible we will 'catch the virtue'; we, too, will become generous and kind people. It is clear that such a 'contagion of virtue' is happening in Uncle Sol's neighborhood. He models as well as teaches the virtues that shape his own life. His stories and poems written for his own children were, in effect, his curriculum, but he embodied his lessons very well. His son, Hank, caught the virtues of kindness and generosity as demonstrated by his interaction with Rocky. And Rocky was in the process of catching the virtues of thoughtfulness and gratitude (among many others) which he displayed when he came to Uncle Sol's home to share pictures and when he thanked Hank for the jacket.

Uncle Sol is encouraged when he sees two of his 'students' beginning to embody the values he has been teaching and modeling for so many years. In a sense, Uncle Sol was 'paying it forward'. His own gratitude for all that people had done for him over the years is expressed in the way that he treats others. After all, how does one repay a teacher for removing the mystery of letters on a page of paper which allows one to discover the world of the written word? How do you repay the stranger in the grocery line who tossed down the extra seventy-nine cents you were short when you got those few items after work? By taking a hint from their embodiment of kindness and generosity and following their lead.

It does not require huge resources to embody virtue or to 'pay it forward'. In Uncle Sol's story which Rocky and Hank read, little Marta had nothing except a desire to give. That desire moved her to share what she could … lilacs. She could not know that the lilacs would have such a profound impact upon her soldier-friend. At the time, he shared the chocolate, but the greater life-long gift he took away from that encounter was to share what he had—whatever it might be in the future—to make another's life brighter, to make the world a more beautiful place.

We are left to wonder if the soldier is Uncle Sol. Whether he is or not, it's clear Uncle Sol has taken to heart the lesson in the story. He looks to make his neighbors' lives brighter and to make the world a more beautiful place in which to live and he does so through giving of himself in his relationships.

Teaching our young to accept their circumstances as challenges with which to forge a life of virtuous integrity is as profound as it is difficult. Yet it is a challenge worth engaging.

Having a mind-set that looks to make the world a more beautiful place, to 'pay it forward,' to express kindness, generosity, self-control and the like would go a long way to making our world a far more pleasant and life-sustaining place.

Questions

1. How would you define a 'good' person? What qualities do they have in their speech, attitudes, behavior?
2. What would be the characteristics of a good citizen in your school? Your community? Your country?
3. What does the phrase mean, "Virtues are caught, not taught"? What kinds of values are you catching in this classroom? What kinds of values are you catching from the media (music, internet, film, print) and "on the street"? Are they all 'virtues'? What is a 'virtue'?
4. Why do you think Uncle Sol is encouraged by what he sees going on between Hank and Rocky?
5. How is your own behavior demonstrating the virtues you have caught? Give an example. Can you think of some virtues you lack and would like to develop? How could you work on that?
6. "Paying it Forward" is not a new idea. Listen to this quote from Benjamin Franklin, "As to the kindness you mention, I wish I could have been of more service to you than I have been, but if I had, the only thanks that I should desire are that you would always be ready to serve any other person that may need your assistance and so let good offices go around, for mankind (humanity) are all of a family. As for my own part, when I am employed in serving others I do not look upon myself as conferring favors but paying debts." How was Dr. Franklin suggesting citizens treat one another? Why did he believe this attitude would be helpful to a society?
7. What small things might you do to make the world a more beautiful place starting today?

CREDITS

They Are The Roses. Words and Music by Randy Van Warmer, Paul Jenkins and Tim Schoeph, Copyright 2002 by Universal Music-A tunes LLC, Eye On The Ball Music Division, Suzabelle Music, Paul Jenkins Songs and Maroon Dogg Music Administered by Universal Music-Z Tunes LLC. International Copyright Secured All Rights Reserved. Reprinted by permission of Hal Leonard Corporation. All Rights for Eye On The Ball Music Division and Suzabelle Music.

Inspiration for "A New Home For Christmas" came from an on-line story by Carol Rehme.

Thanks to Cole Land Transportation Museum in Bangor and especially Galen Cole for his help in creating the image for "Lilacs".

Thanks to Mark Hanks, DVM, for sharing the story of his mother's childhood in postwar Germany.

Inspiration for "Lilacs" came from the life of Robinson "Robby" Speirs (1925-2009) who tried to do something every day of his adult life to make the world a more beautiful place to live.

Thanks to all the children and families of All Souls Church who posed for the illustrations in the book. Although many photos were not used at the time of this publication, each child or group of children represent far more than themselves. They represent the many children past and present who are the roses of All Souls.

Thanks to Mrs. Polly Carlisle for making her yard available for the setting for Uncle Sol's gardens.

Extra special thanks to Carol Sherman, Katie Hall, Beverly Updegraff and FayEllen Haddix for reading galley proofs.

www.ingramcontent.com/pod-product-compliance
Lightning Source LLC
Chambersburg PA
CBHW022109150426
43195CB00008B/338